"John Grimes' delightful cartoons prove that you *can* be a feminist *and* have a wonderful sense of humor."

—Susan Faludi, author
Backlash

"John Grimes catches us unawares—acting human, as we so often do."

—Peter Sussman
San Francisco Chronicle

"Urbane, insightful and just downright funny."

—Pamela Moreland
Marin Independent Journal
Marin County, CA

"John Grimes is a hoot! His sophisticatedly wacky, thoroughly-nineties cartoons are a soothing elixir for tumultuous times."

—Taylor Sisk
The Comic Review
Chapel Hill, NC

"If you love to laugh *and* think at the same time, buy this book! John Grimes' cartoons are wonderfully quirky and jam-packed with lighthearted insights about male/female issues."

—Roz Warren, Editor
Women's Glib and
Mothers! Cartoons by Women
Bala Cynwd, PA

"John Grimes is a fountain of original mirth."

—Jim & Nikki Wood
The Coaster Magazine
Corona del Mar, CA

"John Grimes is a great observer with a gentle spirit. I like the way he sees."

—Teresa Cirolia
The Monthly
Berkeley, CA

"John Grimes always makes me laugh!"

—M.K. Brown, cartoonist
Northern California

"Looking at this wacky collection of cartoons is like holding a mirror to yourself on a bad hair day."

—Glenn Gullmes
San Francisco Comical

"You want to keep worrying about your miserable existence? The put this book down and go over to the *Romantically Dysfunctional New Age Entrepreneur in Search of their Inner Child* section. But if you'd rather go home, lay on the couch and chuckle nonstop, buy John Grimes' book."

—Raymond Lesser
Funny Times
Cleveland, OH

Reality Check

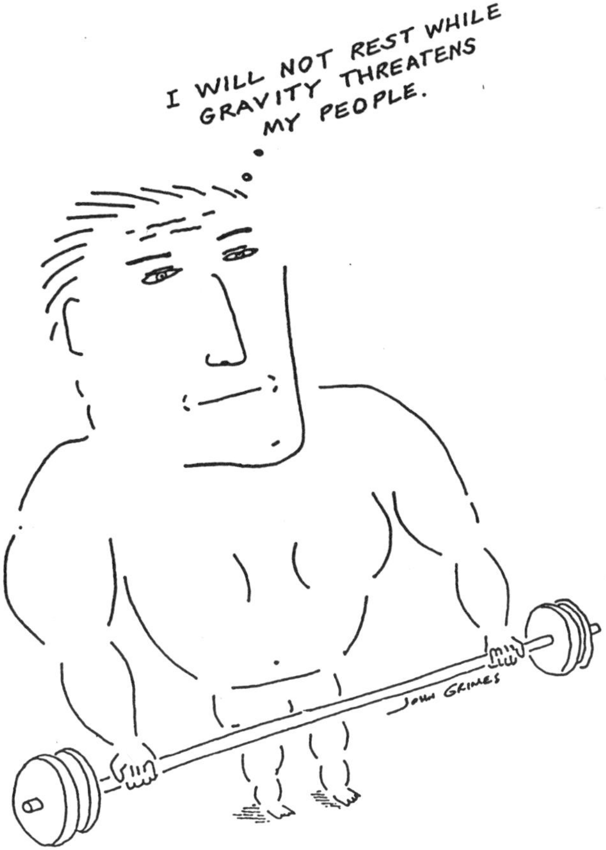
I WILL NOT REST WHILE GRAVITY THREATENS MY PEOPLE.
JOHN GRIMES

by John Grimes

Ten Speed Press

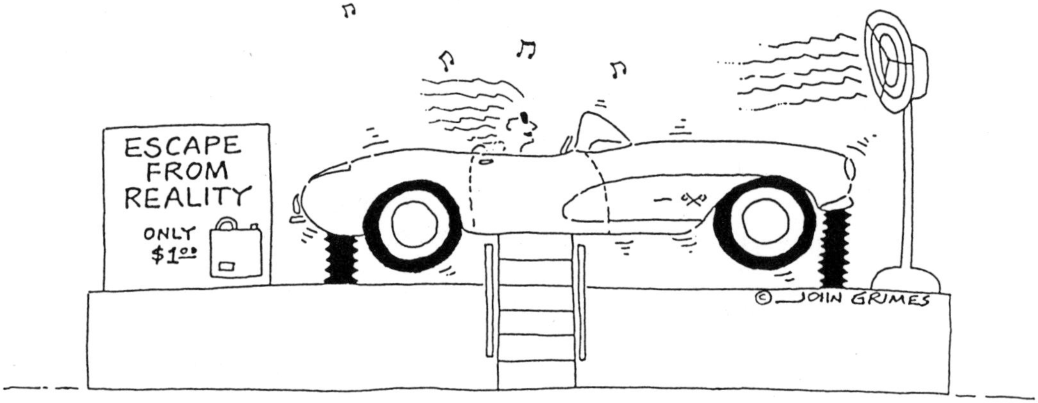
ESCAPE
FROM
REALITY
ONLY
$1.00
© JOHN GRIMES

Library of Congress Cataloging-in-Publication Data:

Grimes, John, 1947–
Reality check : cartoons / by John Grimes
p. cm.
ISBN 0-89815-544-4
1. United States—Social life and customs—Caricatures and cartoons. 2. Pictorial wit and humor. American. I. Title.
NC1429.G722A4 1993 93-12849
741.5'973—dc20 CIP

Published by Ten Speed Press, P.O. Box 7123, Berkeley, California 94707

Printed in the United States of America
1 2 3 4 5—97 96 95 94 93

I dedicate this book, with love, to
Robin Chin,
my inspiration and alter (if not *altar*) ego.

With bountiful thanks to
Barbara Ames,
my mother—a wonderfully funny Renaissance woman;
to David Grimes, my late father—a gentle man, who would have been proud;
to my lighthearted siblings: Susie, Kathy, Dave, Molly and Andy,
and their families of merrymakers;
and to Robin's family, for withholding judgment on my sanity...

to the clever and thoughtful David Jouris;
the inspirational SARK;
the wondrous Patty "Words Are My Language" Warren;
the amusing and cerebral John & Ann Carroll;
the "Bull Goose Loonie" Barry Gantt;
and to Dan Steven, the Schlegels, the Hulls,
David Povilaitis, Judith Black and Jeff Pieplow—
each as witty as the next...

to Phil Wood, Fuzzy Randall and George Young at Ten Speed Press,
for laughing all the way to *my* bank (and to my agents,
Laurie Fox and Linda Chester, for illuminating the way)...

to Peter Sussman
of the *San Francisco Chronicle*, for his early and continued support;
Pamela Moreland and Barbara Morgan of the *Marin Independent Journal*;
Teresa Cirolia and Andreas Jones of *The Monthly*;
and to other editors and art directors who've encouraged my quirkiness.

Special thanks to the enlightened folks (in day-job land) at
Peachpit Press and Goldstein & Blair (especially Ted Nace and Arthur Naiman),
for supporting my cartooning habit...

and to other friends and enthusiasts,
whose chortles made me want to sit down and do more.

Last but not least, thanks to you—funloving, fully-evolved readers.

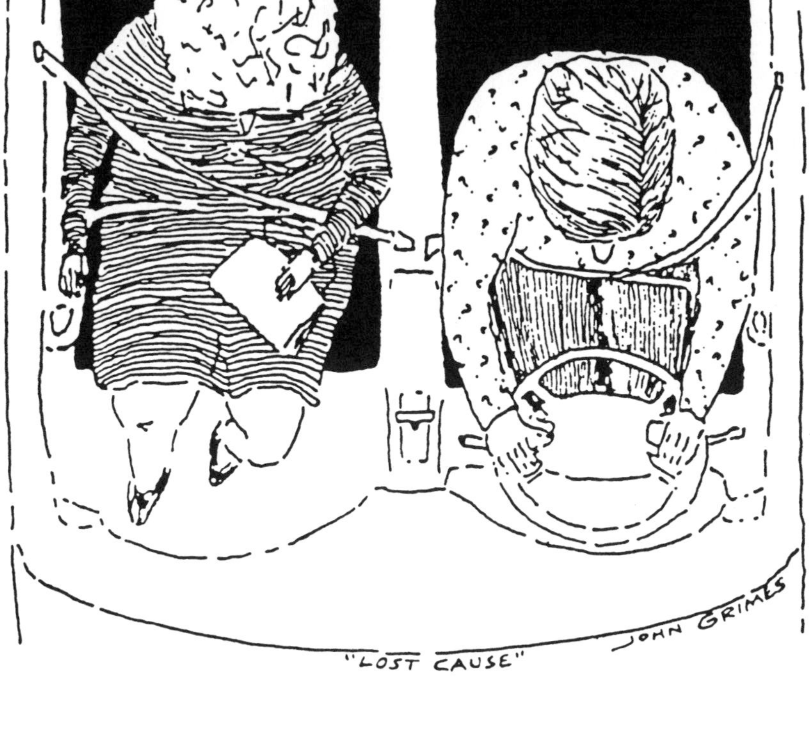
HENRY, WE'RE LOST! WHY KEEP DRIVING AROUND?
MARTHA, A MAN'S GOTTA DO WHAT A MAN'S GOTTA DO.
JOHN GRIMES
"LOST CAUSE"

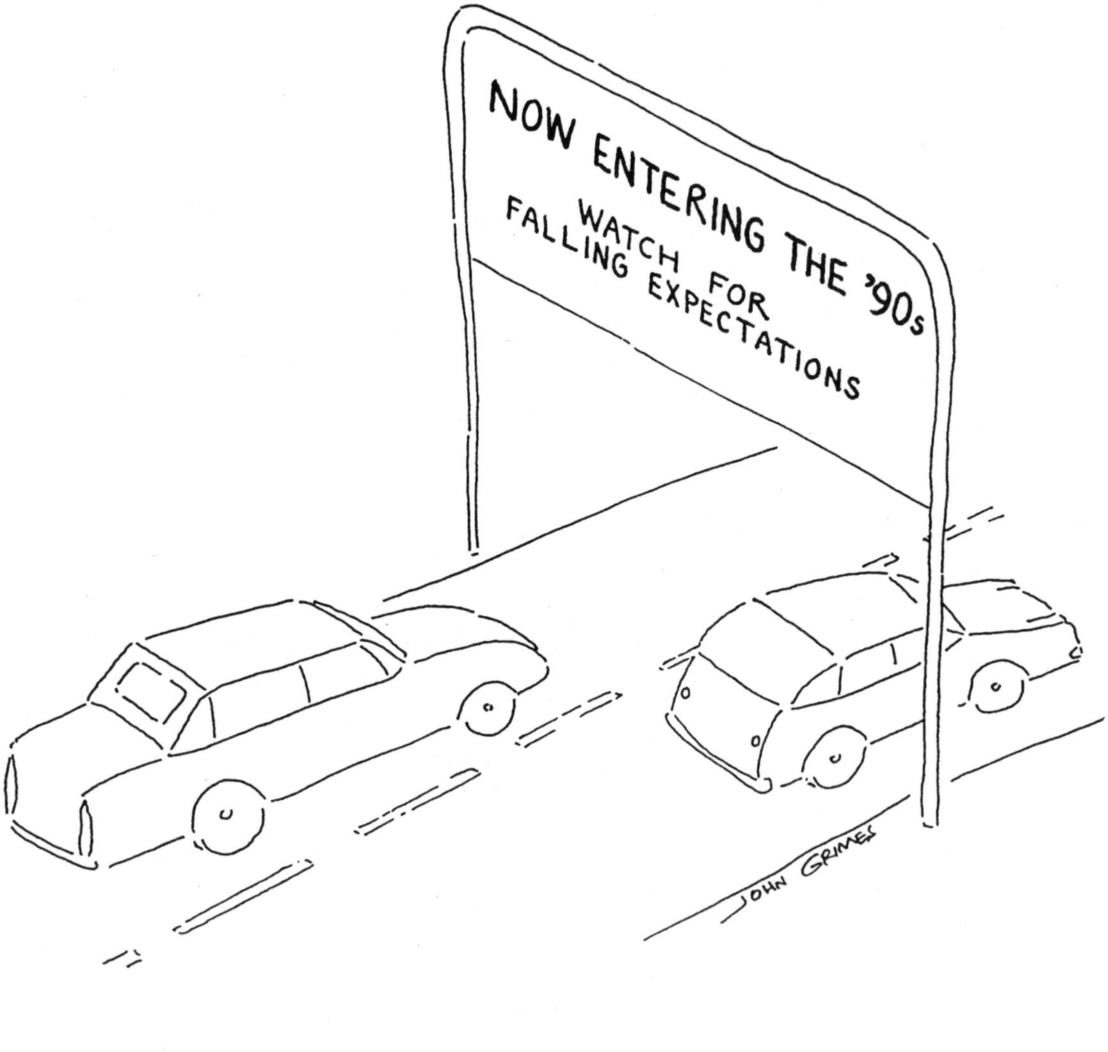
NOW ENTERING THE '90s
WATCH FOR
FALLING EXPECTATIONS
JOHN GRIMES

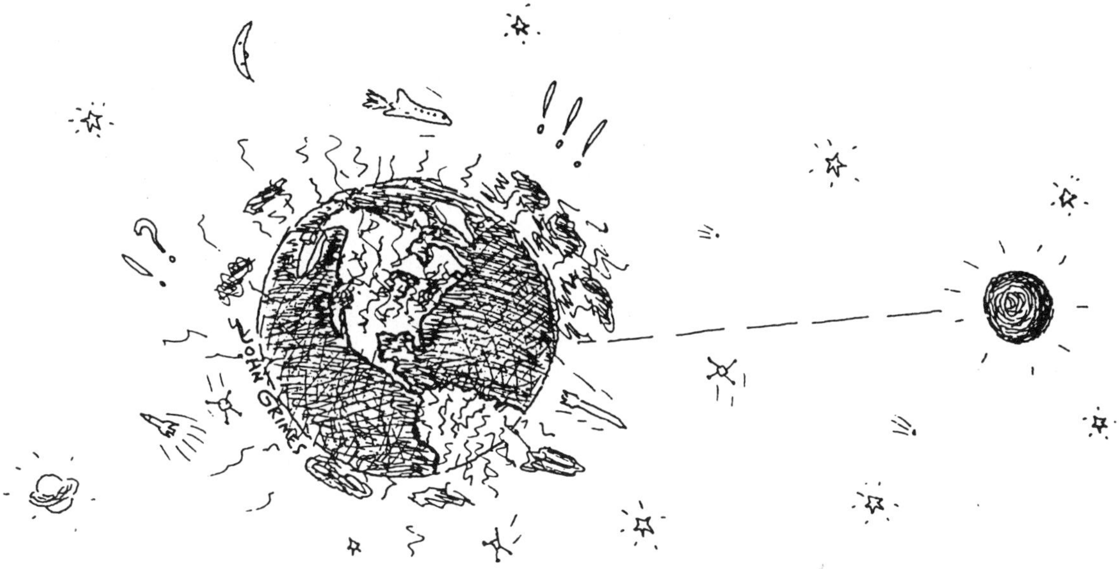
JOHN GRIMES

OVERWHELMED BY INCONSIDERATE INHABITANTS,
EARTH DEVELOPS A SERIOUS CASE OF
VENUS ENVY.

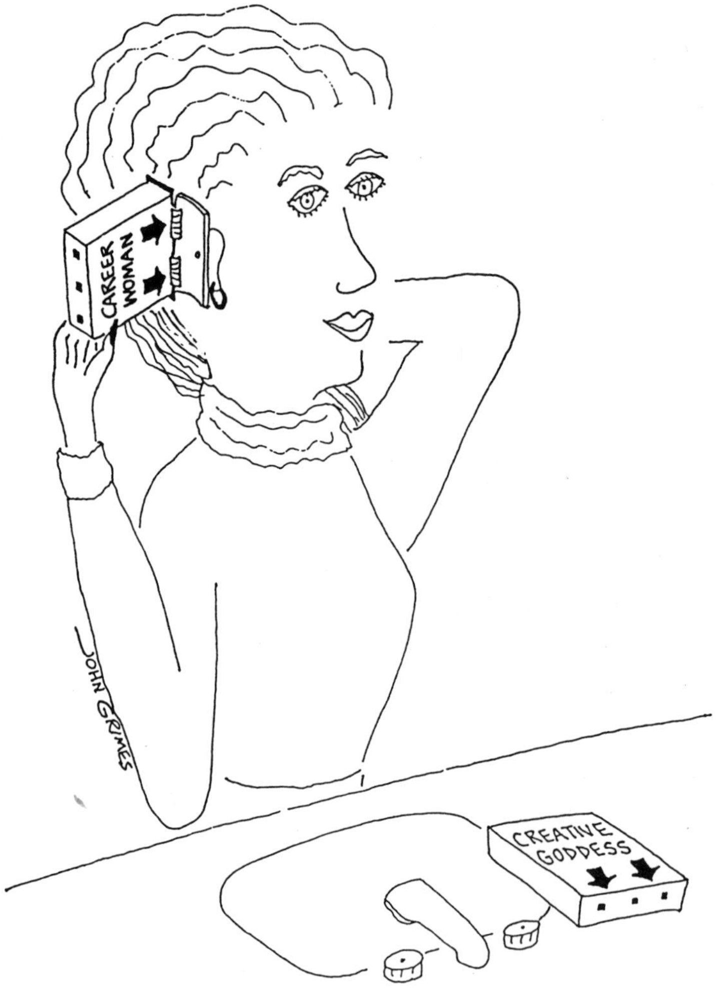
CAREER WOMAN
JOHN GRIMES
CREATIVE GODDESS

JUST BEFORE WORK, JEANIE WOULD SLIP INTO THE LADIES ROOM AND ADJUST HER PERSONALITY.

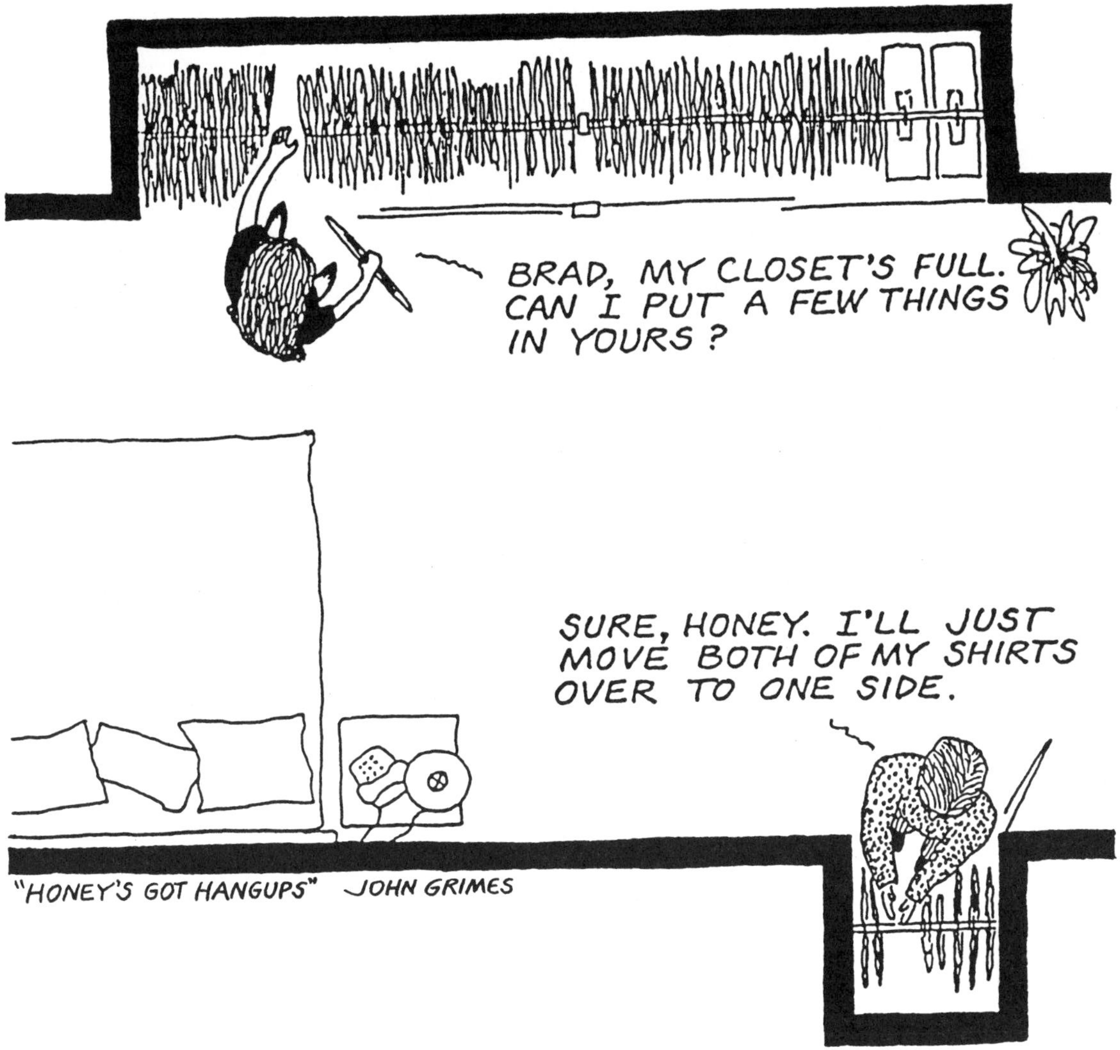
BRAD, MY CLOSET'S FULL. CAN I PUT A FEW THINGS IN YOURS?
SURE, HONEY. I'LL JUST MOVE BOTH OF MY SHIRTS OVER TO ONE SIDE.
"HONEY'S GOT HANGUPS" JOHN GRIMES

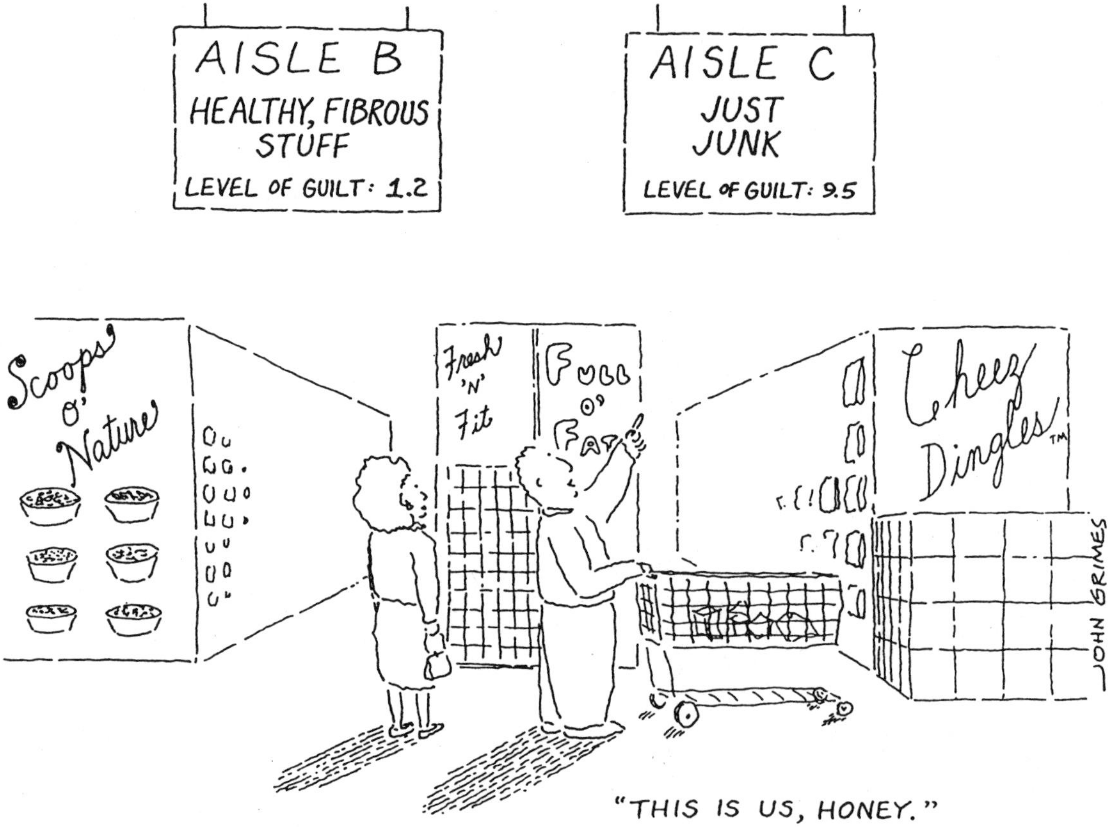
AISLE B
HEALTHY, FIBROUS STUFF
LEVEL OF GUILT: 1.2
AISLE C
JUST JUNK
LEVEL OF GUILT: 9.5
Scoops O' Nature
Fresh 'N' Fit
Chez Dingles TM
JOHN GRIMES

"THIS IS US, HONEY."

Hi, Bob, this is your biological voicemail. For messages from your stomach, blink once... from your conscience, blink twice... and from your plumbing, three times...
WHILE I WAS OUT
JOHN GRIMES

INSTANT INTEGRITY
For people too busy to develop their own

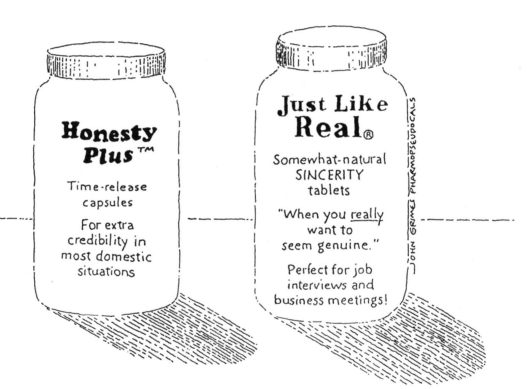

Honesty Plus™

Time-release
capsules

For extra
credibility in
most domestic
situations

Just Like Real®

Somewhat-natural
SINCERITY
tablets

"When you really
want to
seem genuine."

Perfect for job
interviews and
business meetings!

JOHN GRIMES PHARMOPSEUDOCALS

KEVIN, THE TESTS CAME BACK POSITIVE.
I'M AFRAID YOU'RE A JERK.

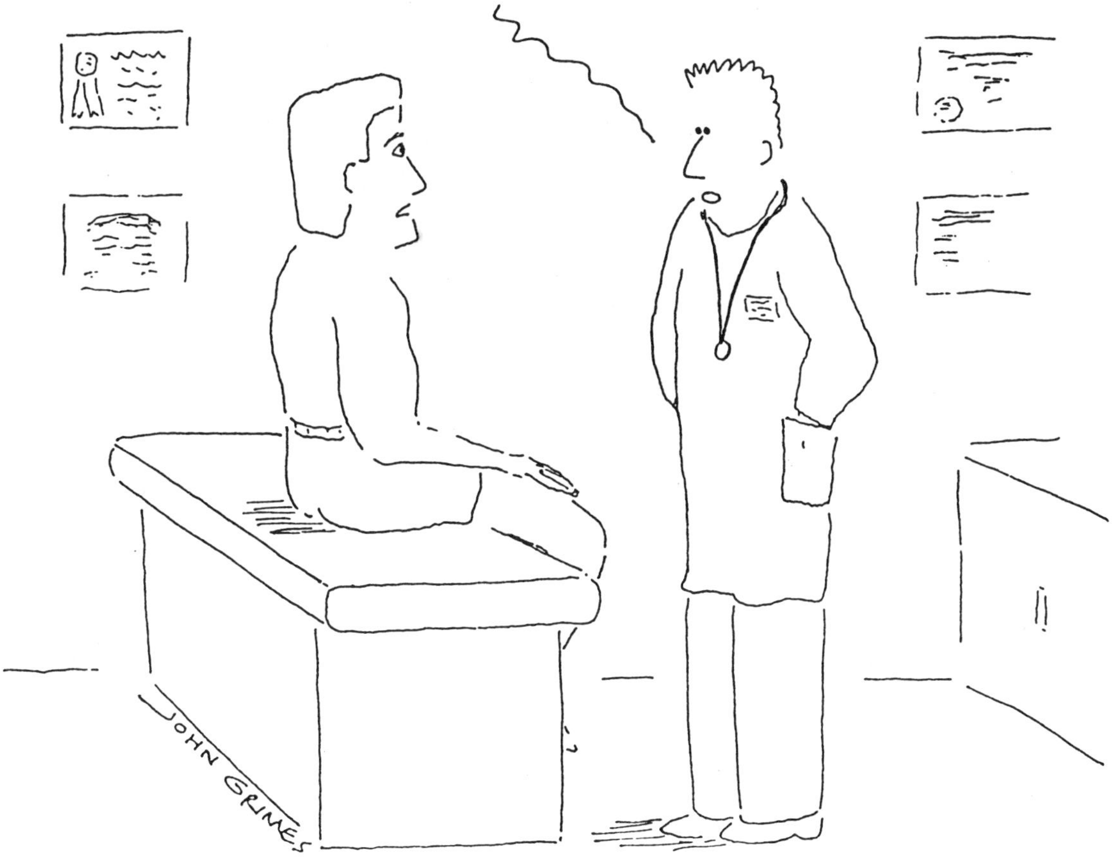
JOHN GRIMES

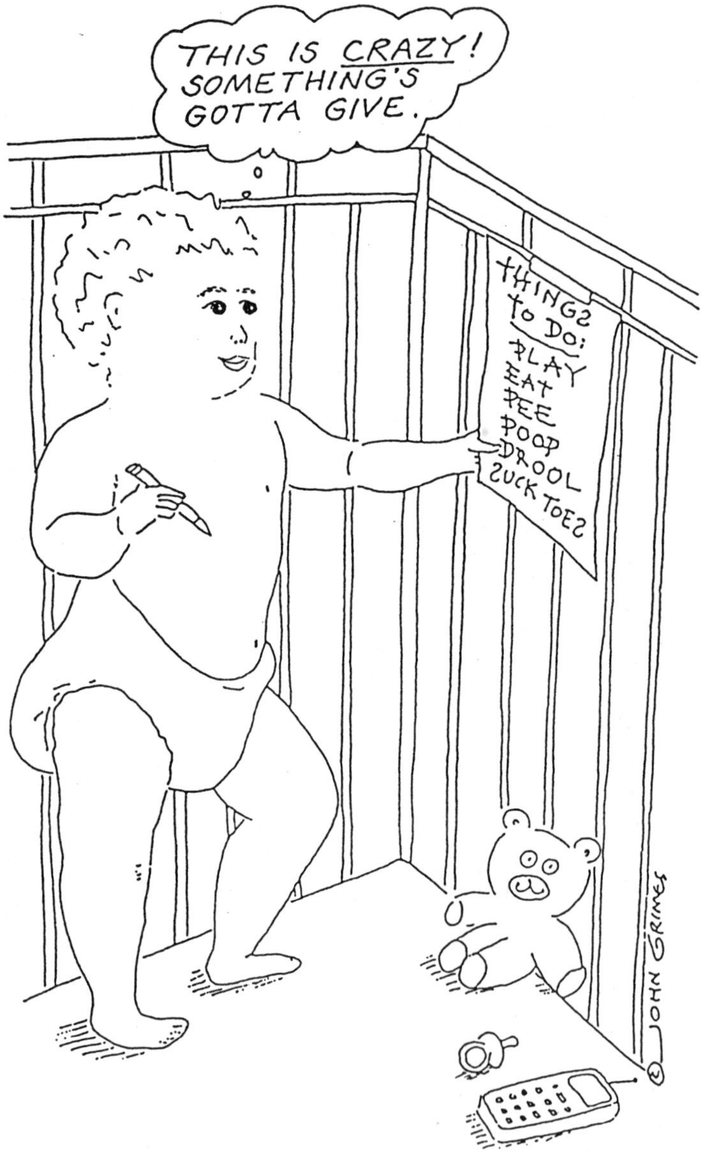
THIS IS CRAZY! SOMETHING'S GOTTA GIVE.
THINGS TO DO:
PLAY
EAT
PEE
POOP
DROOL
SUCK TOES
© JOHN GRIMES

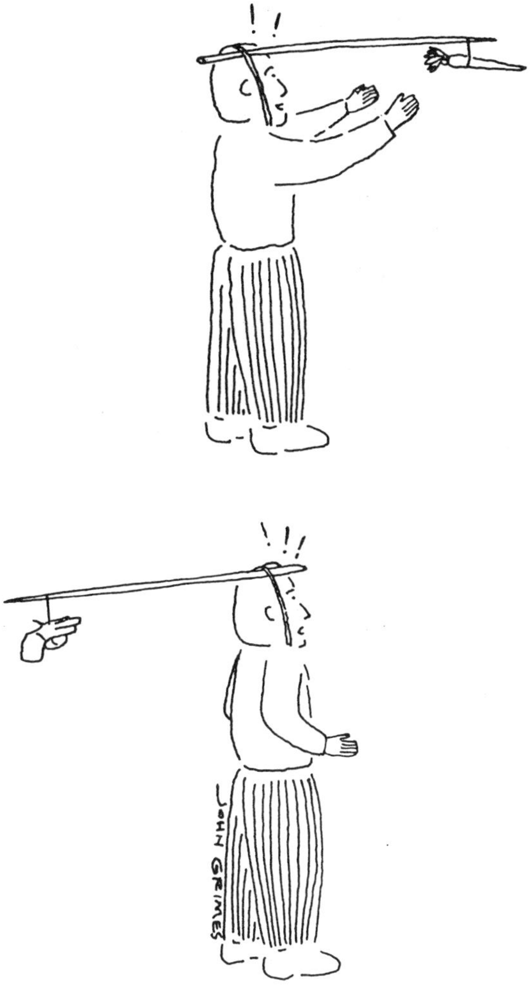
JOHN GRIMES

MOTIVATION

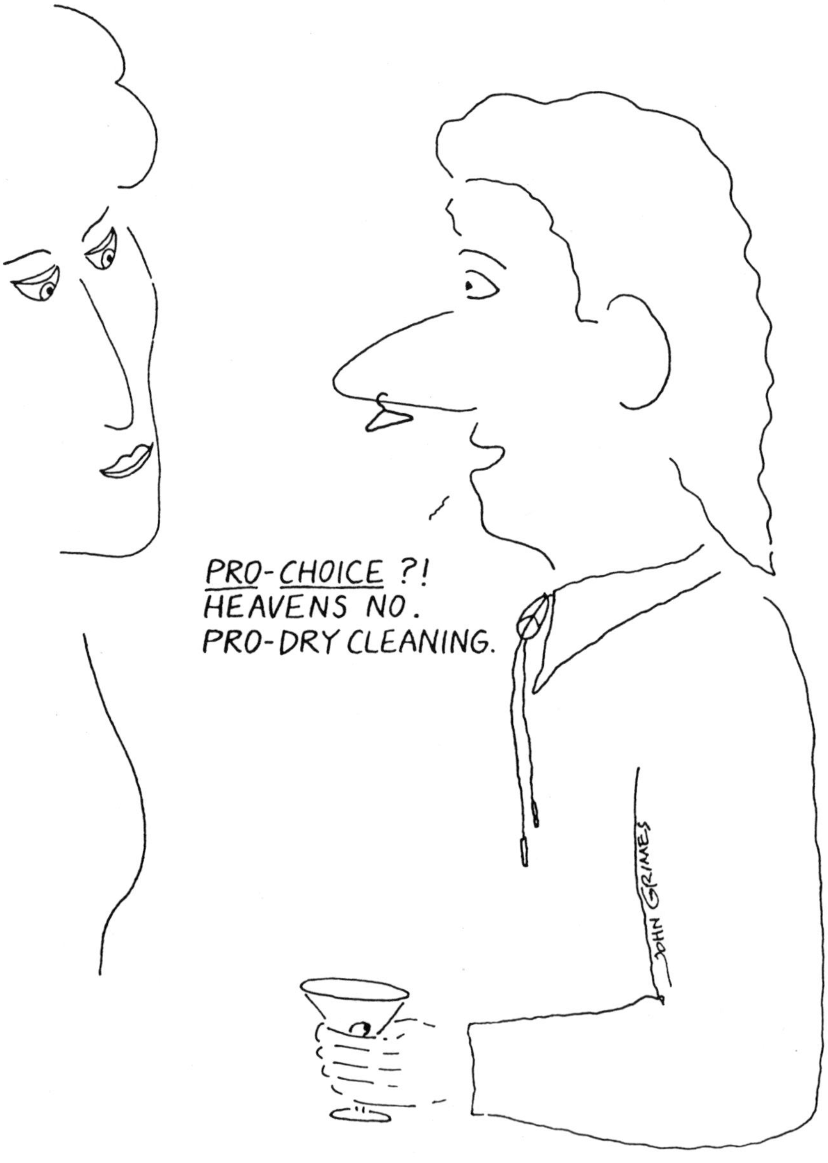
PRO-CHOICE ?! HEAVENS NO. PRO-DRY CLEANING.
JOHN GRIMES

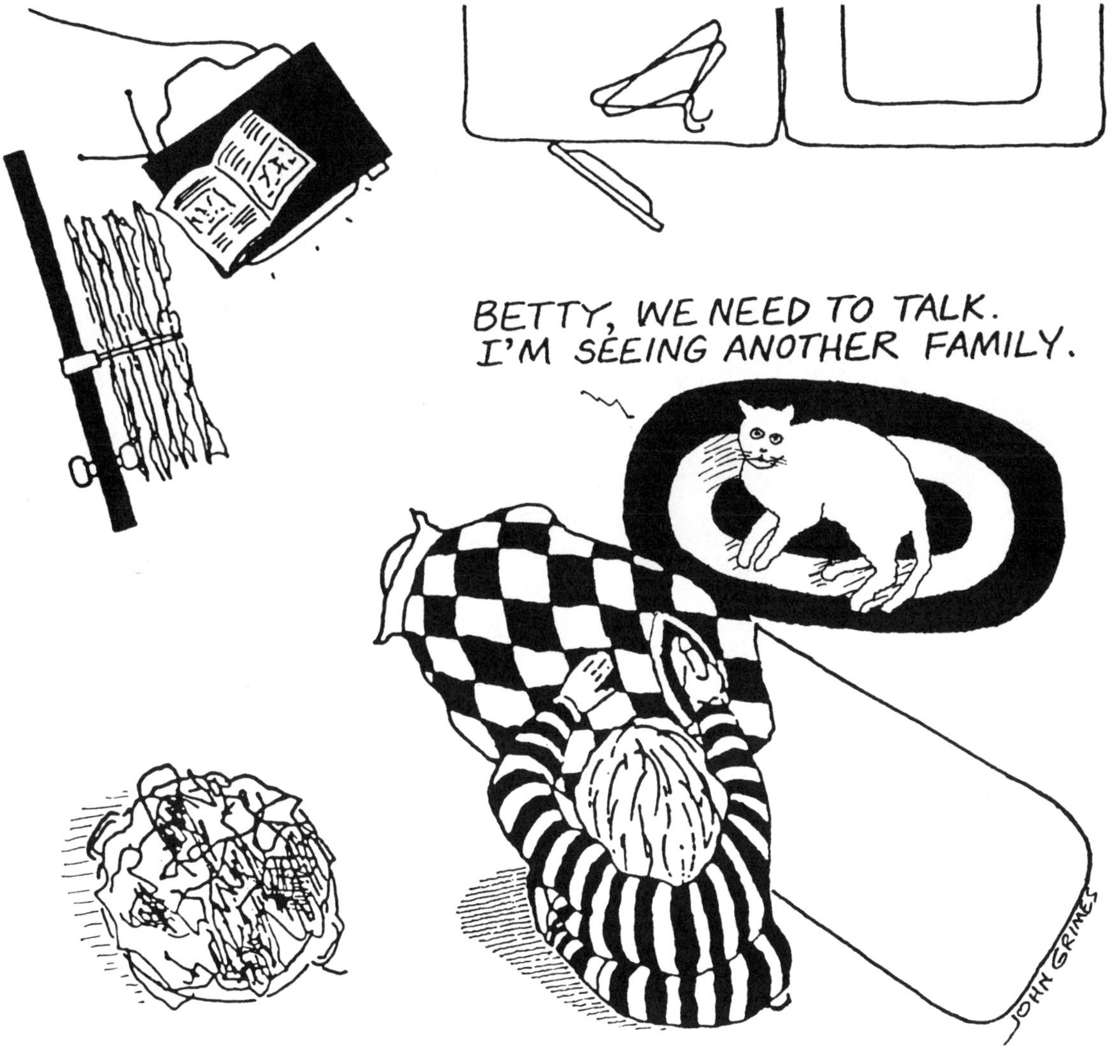
BETTY, WE NEED TO TALK.
I'M SEEING ANOTHER FAMILY.
JOHN GRIMES

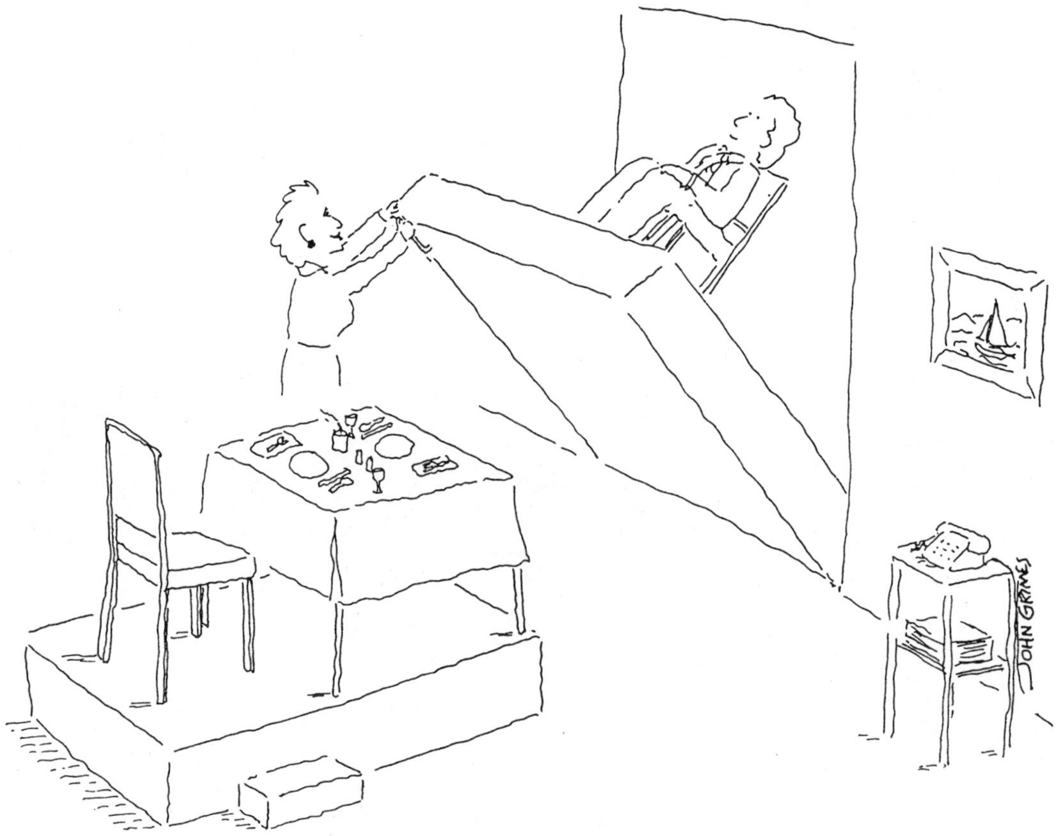
JOHN GRIMES

WEARY OF THE DATING GAME,
BETH INVESTS IN A MURPHY-MAN.™

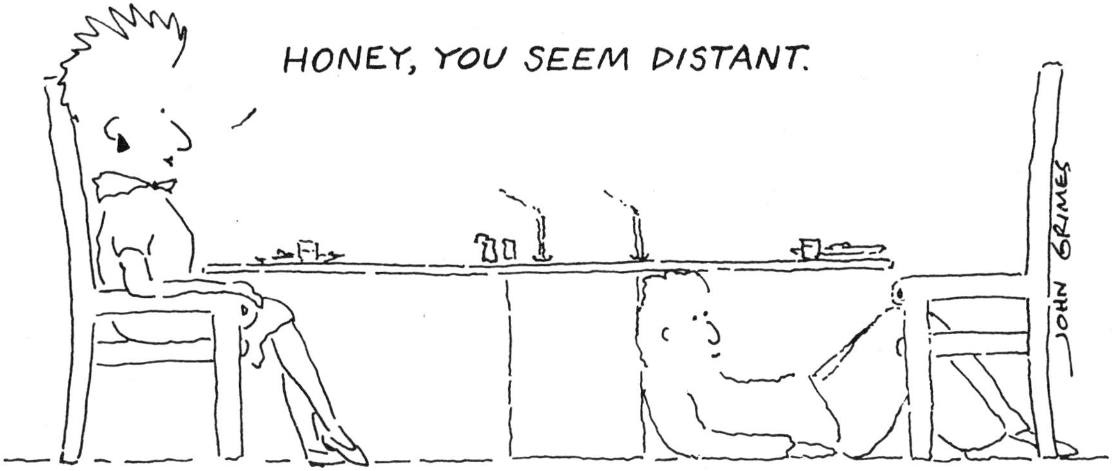
HONEY, YOU SEEM DISTANT.
JOHN GRIMES

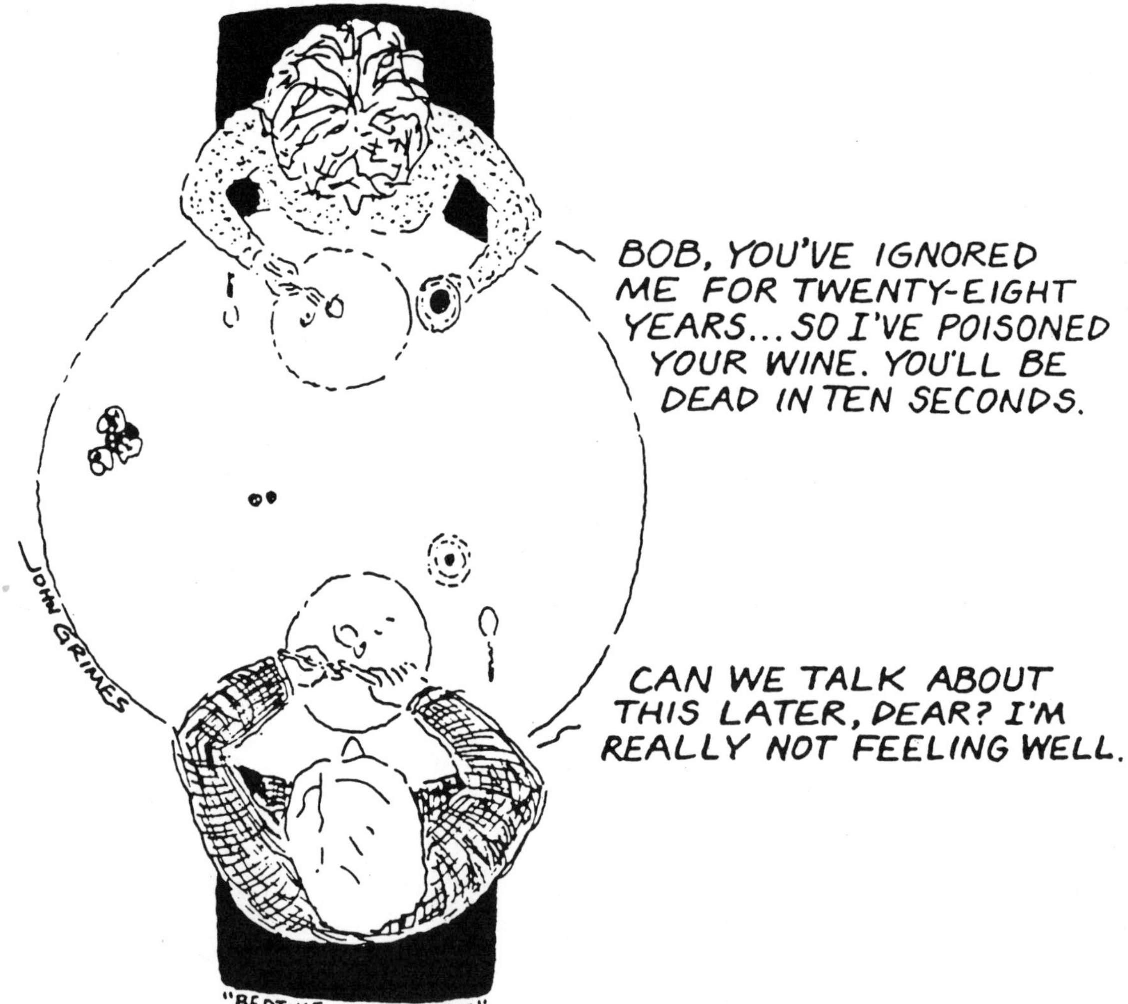
BOB, YOU'VE IGNORED ME FOR TWENTY-EIGHT YEARS... SO I'VE POISONED YOUR WINE. YOU'LL BE DEAD IN TEN SECONDS.
CAN WE TALK ABOUT THIS LATER, DEAR? I'M REALLY NOT FEELING WELL.
JOHN GRIMES

"BEDTIME FOR BOBBY"

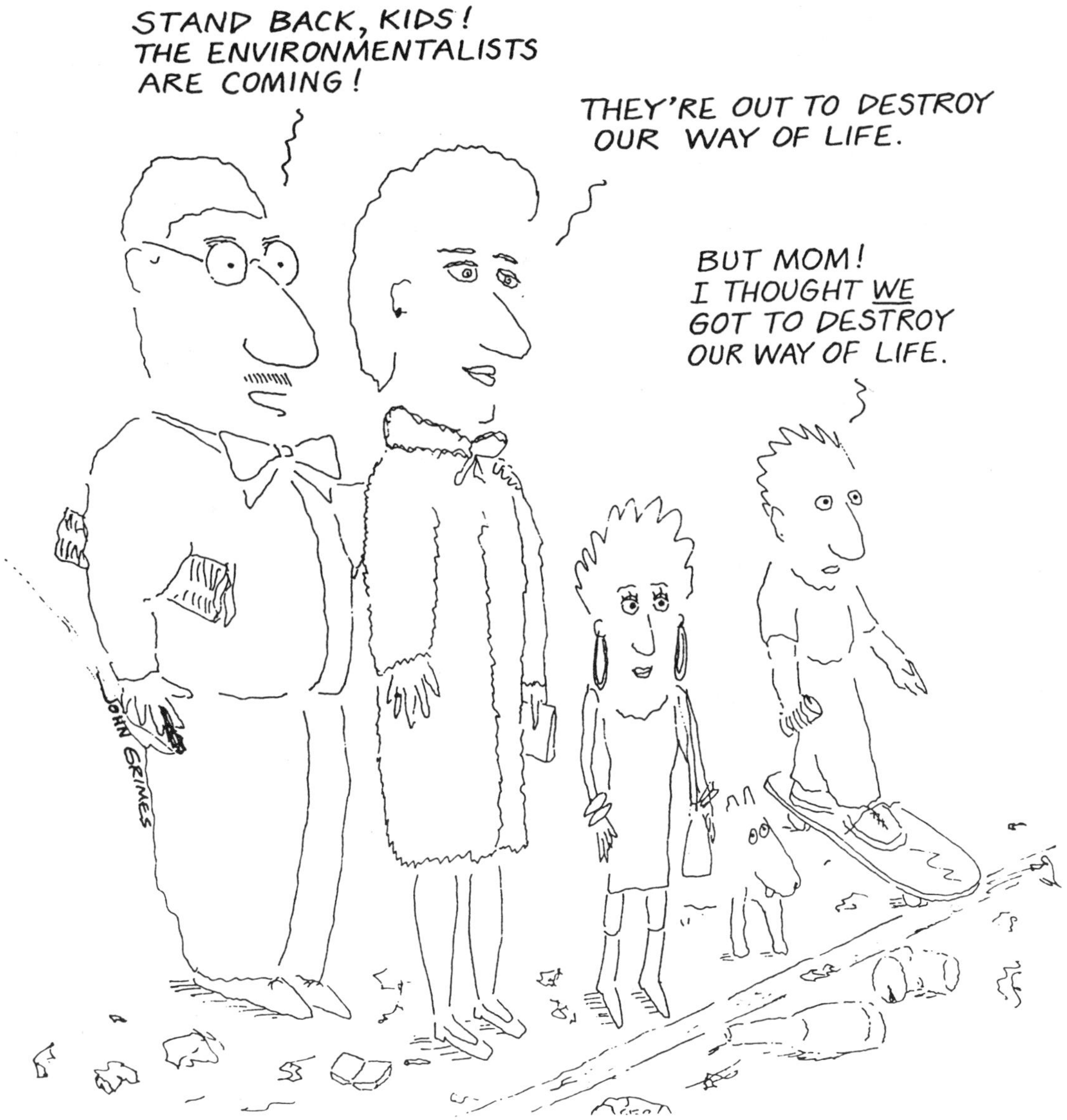
STAND BACK, KIDS! THE ENVIRONMENTALISTS ARE COMING!
THEY'RE OUT TO DESTROY OUR WAY OF LIFE.
BUT MOM! I THOUGHT WE GOT TO DESTROY OUR WAY OF LIFE.
JOHN GRIMES

IT'S ALL YOURS SON.
YOU SHOULDN'T HAVE.
HEALTH CARE SYSTEM
HOMELESS
Greed
WAR
ENVIRONMENTAL
EXPLOITATION
JOHN GRIMES

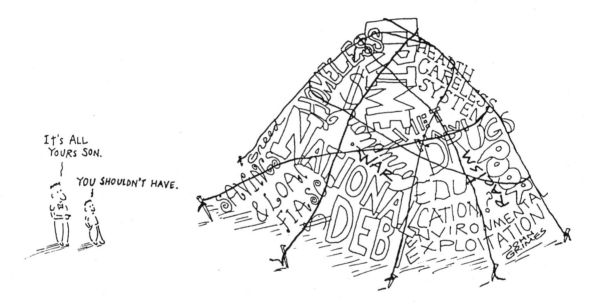

BOB, WE SEEM TO BE DRIFTING APART.
INTERESTING THEORY, SUSAN. LET ME GET BACK TO YOU.
JOHN GRIMES

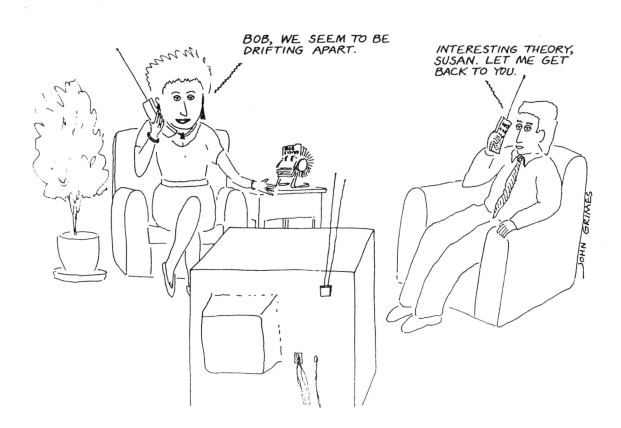

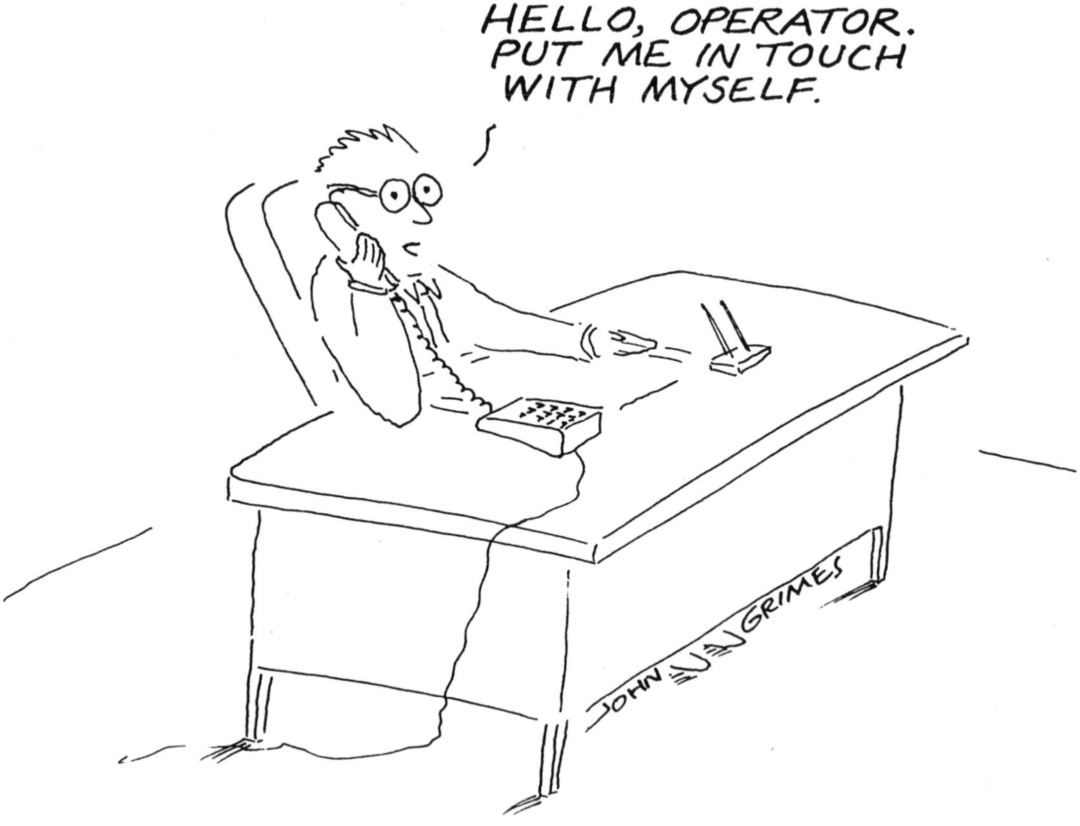
HELLO, OPERATOR.
PUT ME IN TOUCH
WITH MYSELF.
JOHN GRIMES

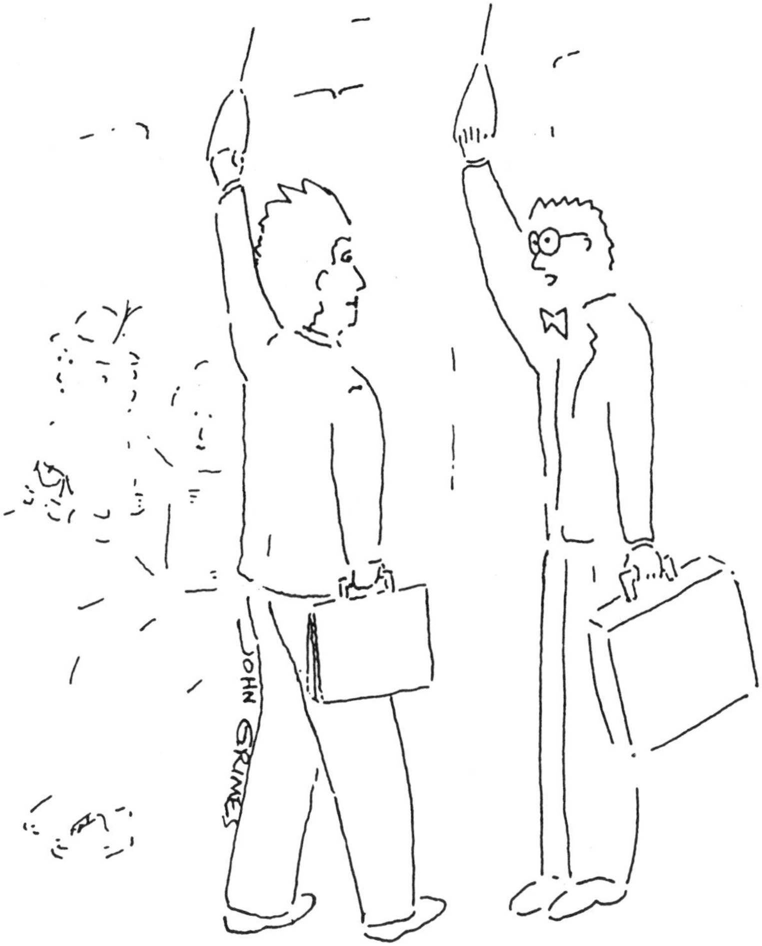
JOHN GRIMES

C'MON MIKE, WOULD THE DOLPHINS GIVE UP THEIR FAVORITE SANDWICH TO SAVE OUR BUTTS?

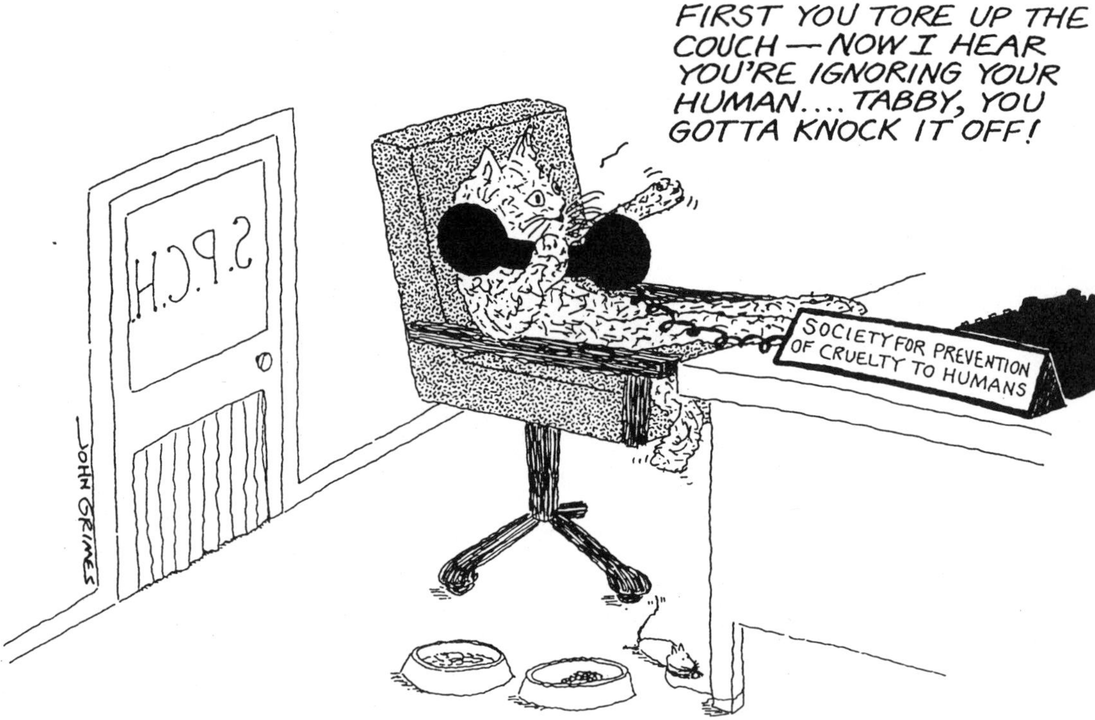
FIRST YOU TORE UP THE COUCH — NOW I HEAR YOU'RE IGNORING YOUR HUMAN.... TABBY, YOU GOTTA KNOCK IT OFF!
S.P.C.H.
SOCIETY FOR PREVENTION OF CRUELTY TO HUMANS
JOHN GRIMES

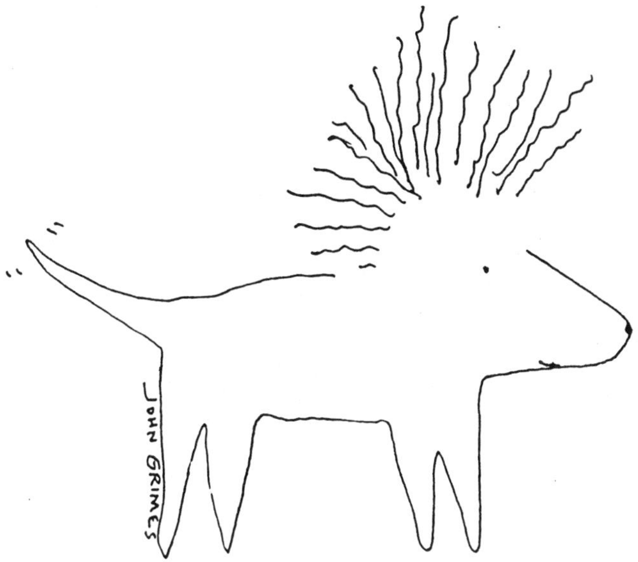
JOHN GRIMES

DON KING DOG

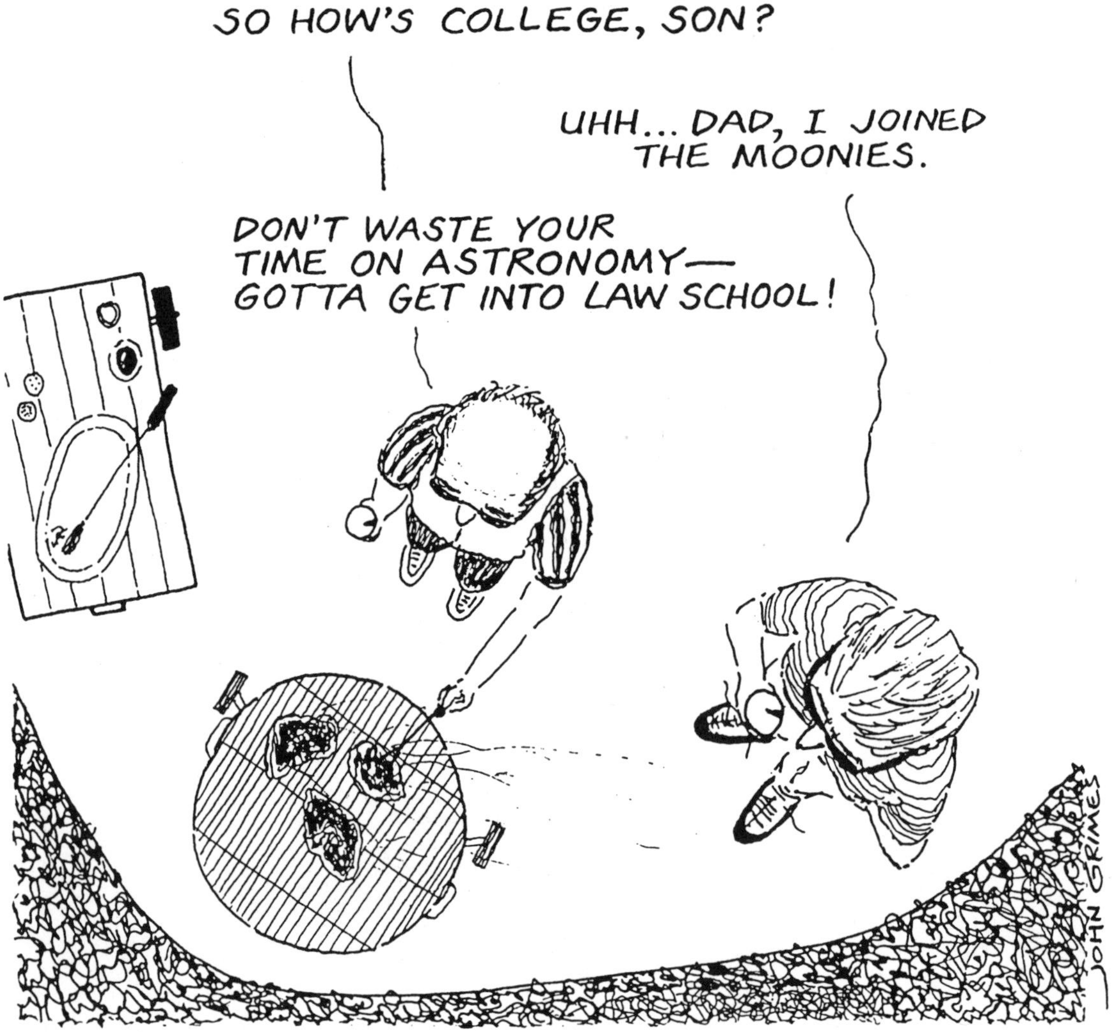
SO HOW'S COLLEGE, SON?
DON'T WASTE YOUR TIME ON ASTRONOMY— GOTTA GET INTO LAW SCHOOL!
UHH... DAD, I JOINED THE MOONIES.
JOHN GRIMES

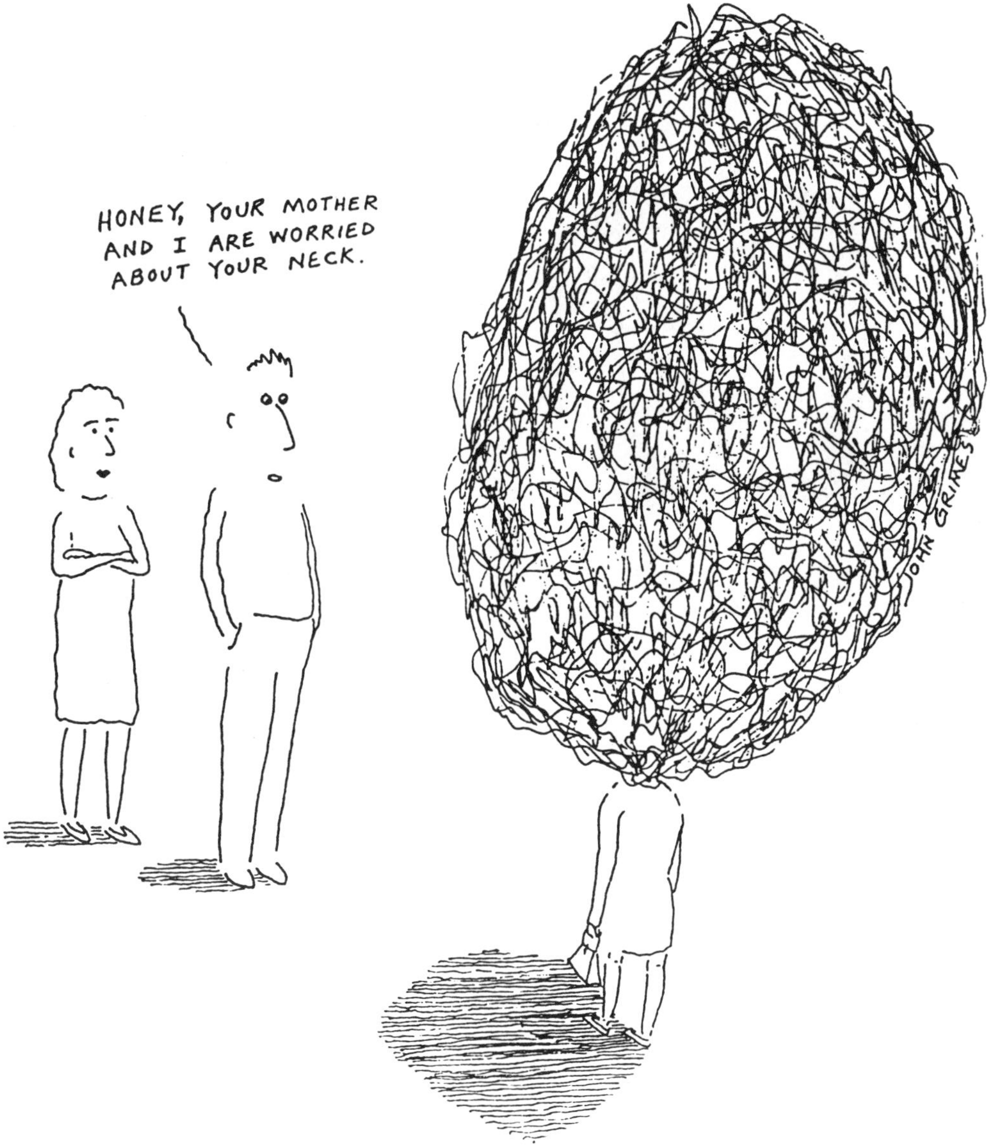
HONEY, YOUR MOTHER AND I ARE WORRIED ABOUT YOUR NECK.
JOHN GRIMES

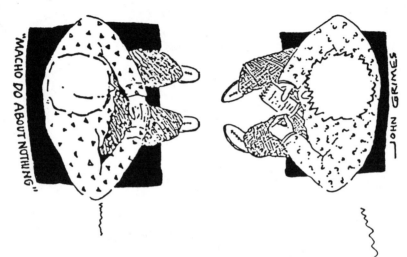

"MACHO DO ABOUT NOTHING."
JOHN GRIMES
DOC, MY WIFE KEEPS NAGGING ME TO DO HOUSEWORK AND SPEND TIME WITH HER AND THE KIDS.
IS THAT UNFAIR?
ARE YOU KIDDING? I HAVEN'T HAD AN EXTRA MINUTE SINCE WE GOT CABLE.

Betty's OBEDIENCE SCHOOL for MEN
CONVERSE, PHIL, CONVERSE.
OK, ONCE MORE WITH FEELING: "AND HOW WAS YOUR DAY, HONEY?"
FRED, THIS MAY SCARE YOU AT FIRST. IT'S CALLED "INTIMACY."
JOHN GRIMES

FAMOUS CROSS-DRESSERS

DR. JEKYLL   MRS. HYDE

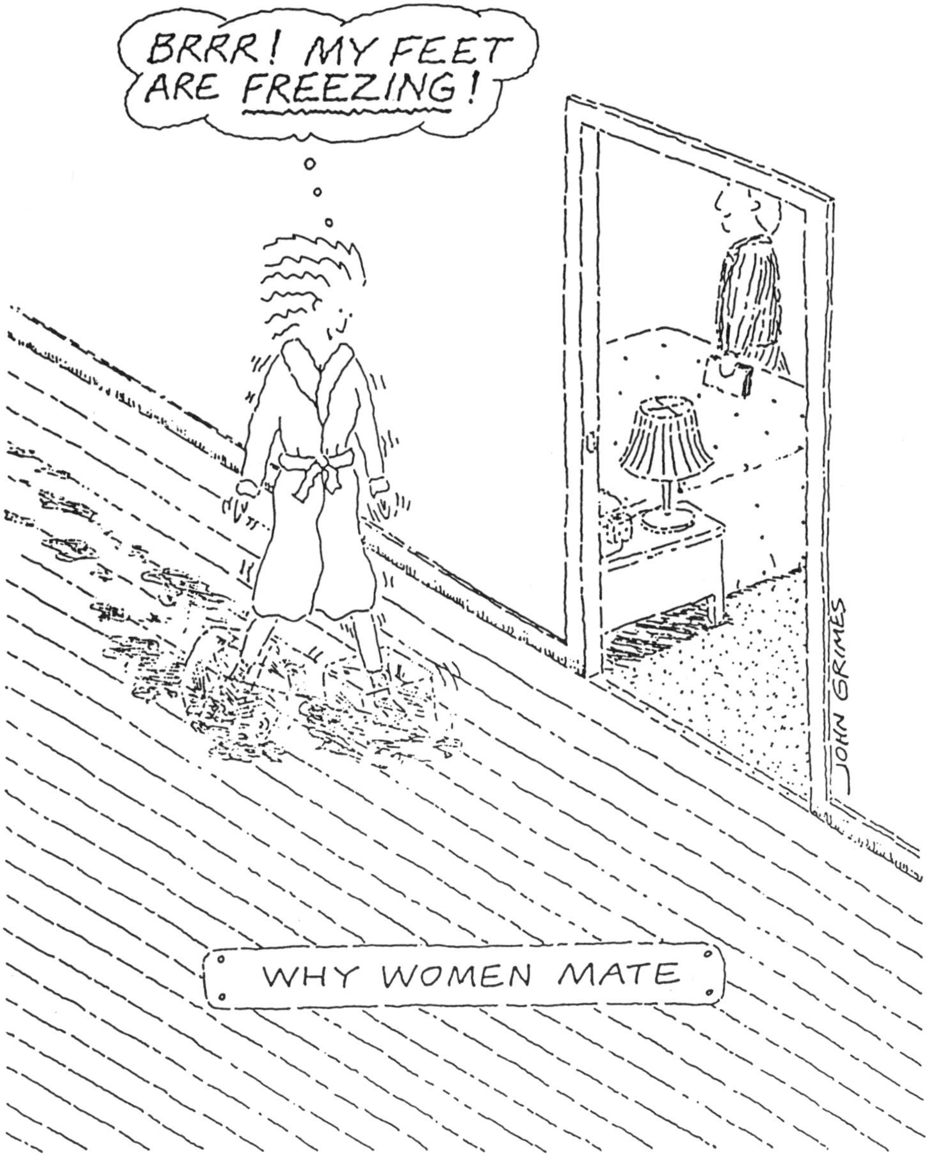
BRRR! MY FEET ARE FREEZING!
JOHN GRIMES
WHY WOMEN MATE

INTRODUCING
BOAST-IT NOTES!™
MINE'S BIGGER THAN YOURS!
DON'T HATE ME BECAUSE I'M BEAUTIFUL.
I'VE BEEN A SIZE 6 SINCE HIGH SCHOOL!
THE BOSS SAYS I'M LIKE FAMILY.
JOHN GRIMES
BRAG A LITTLE WITH OUR SELF-STICK PADS OF SELF-ESTEEM!
I LOVE MENSA MEETINGS

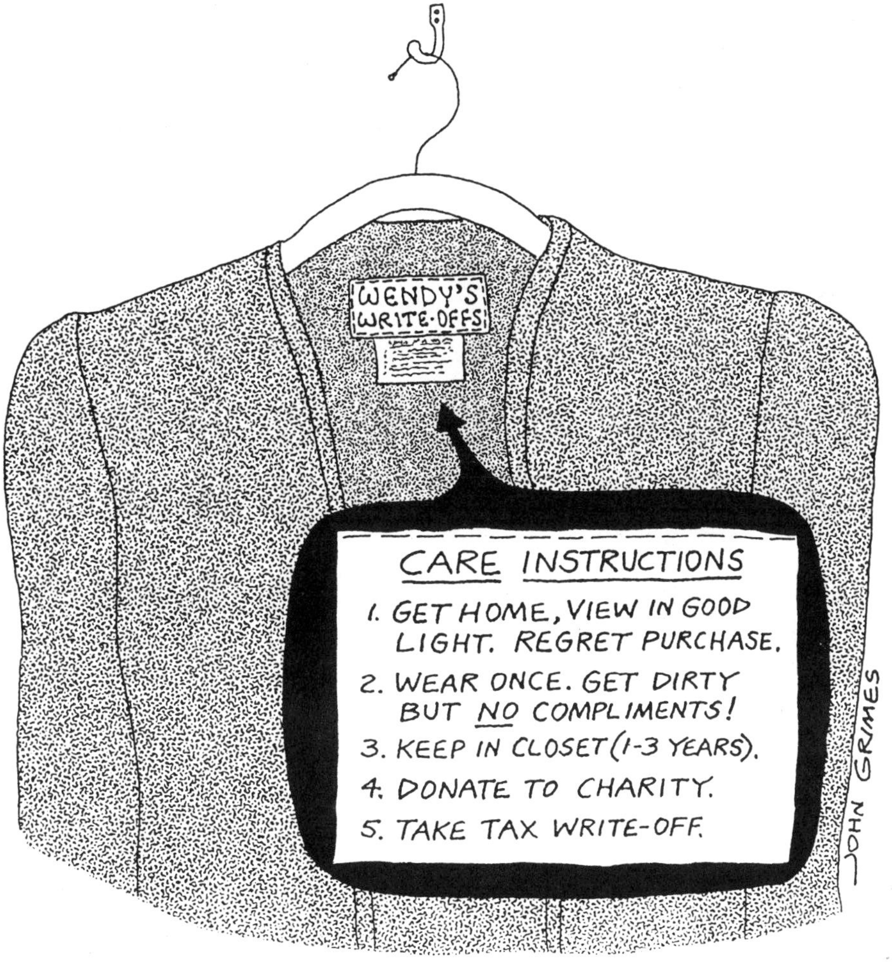
WENDY'S WRITE-OFFS
CARE INSTRUCTIONS
1. GET HOME, VIEW IN GOOD LIGHT. REGRET PURCHASE.
2. WEAR ONCE. GET DIRTY BUT NO COMPLIMENTS!
3. KEEP IN CLOSET (1-3 YEARS).
4. DONATE TO CHARITY.
5. TAKE TAX WRITE-OFF.
JOHN GRIMES

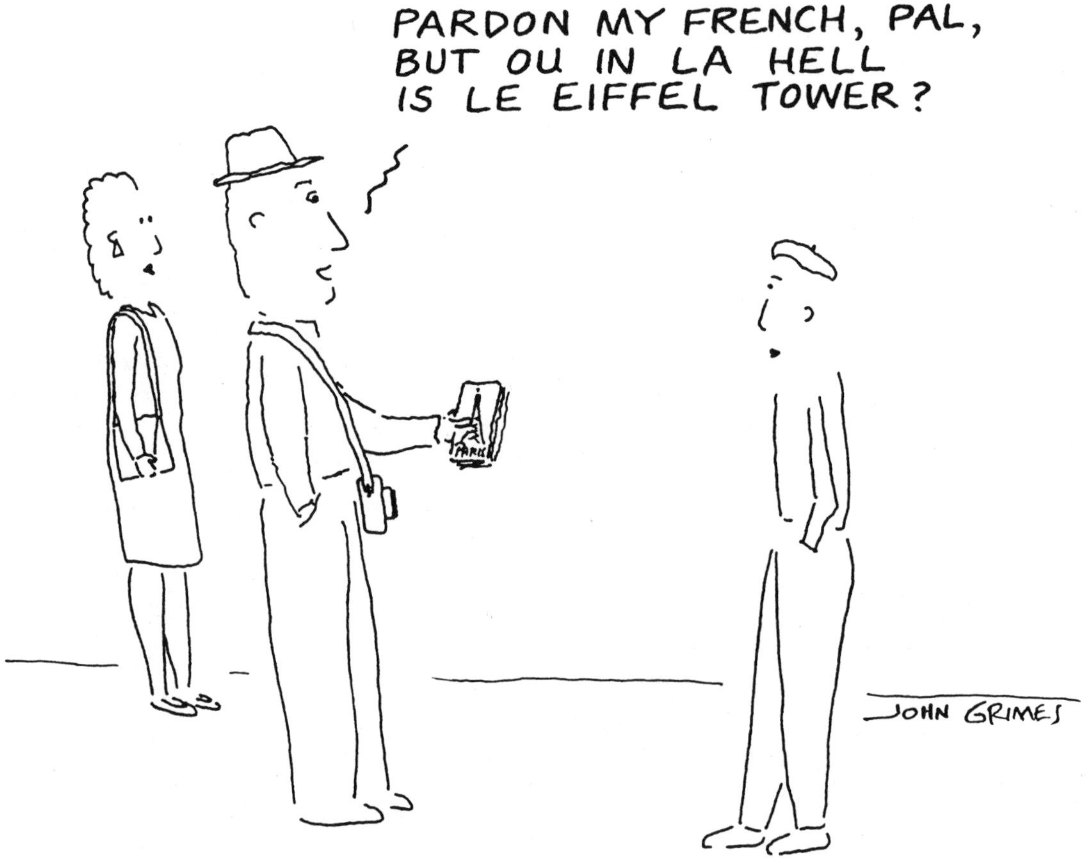
PARDON MY FRENCH, PAL, BUT OU IN LA HELL IS LE EIFFEL TOWER?
JOHN GRIMES

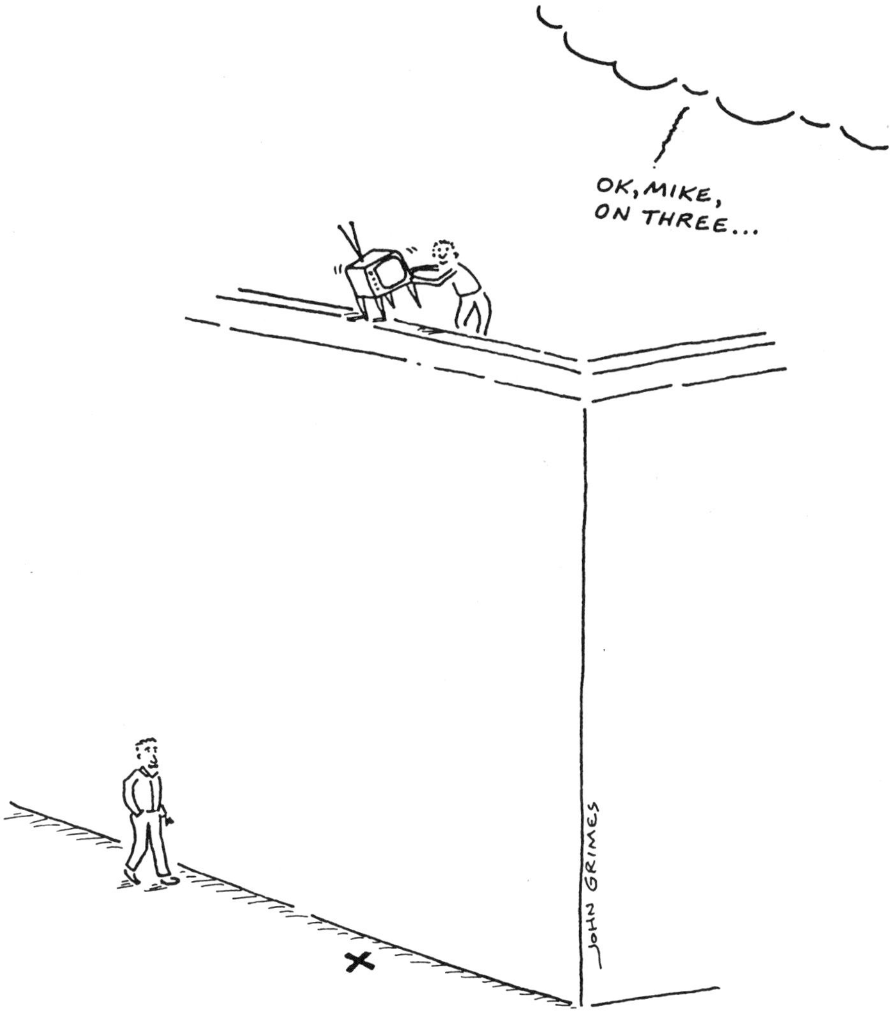
OK, MIKE,
ON THREE...
JOHN GRIMES

GERALDO RIVERA
ABOUT TO BE KILLED
BY AN ACT OF GOD

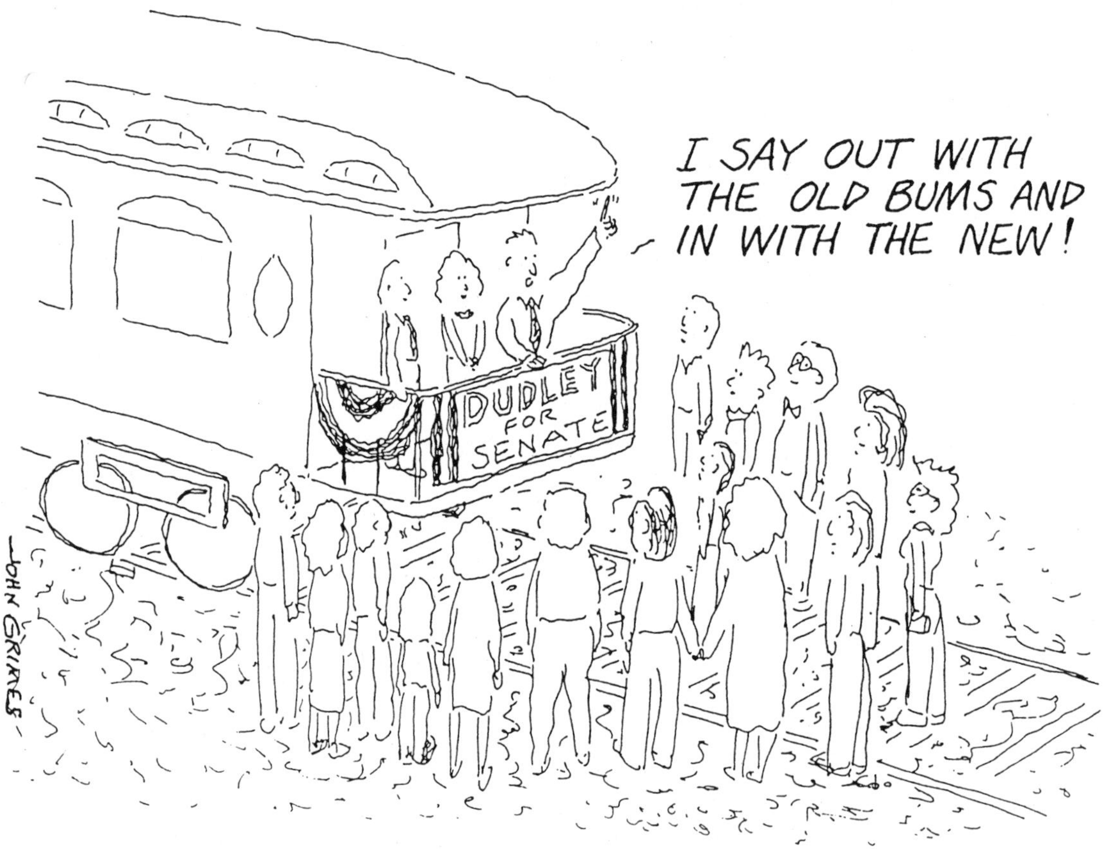
I SAY OUT WITH THE OLD BUMS AND IN WITH THE NEW!
DUDLEY FOR SENATE
JOHN GRIMES

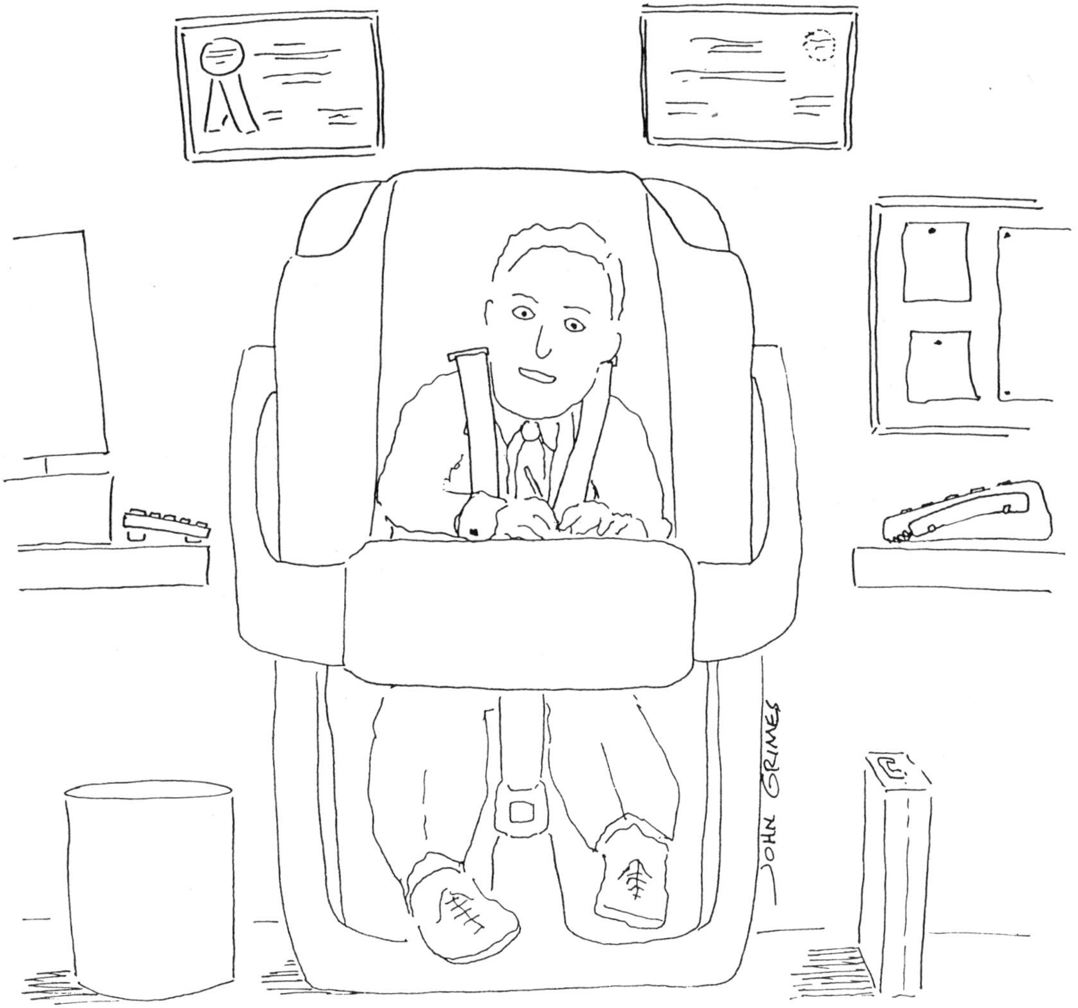
JOHN GRIMES

CORPORATE SAFETY SEAT
FOR RIDING OUT THE RECESSION

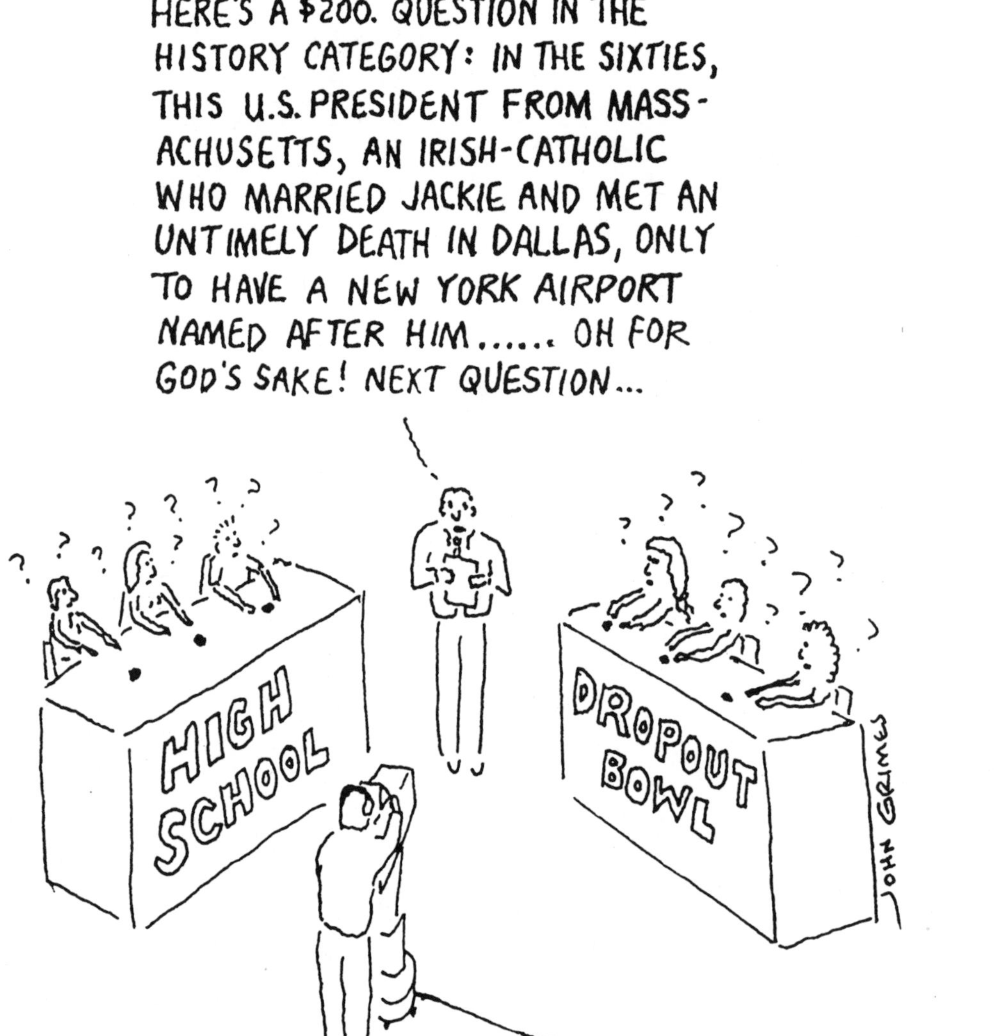
HERE'S A $200. QUESTION IN THE HISTORY CATEGORY: IN THE SIXTIES, THIS U.S. PRESIDENT FROM MASS-ACHUSETTS, AN IRISH-CATHOLIC WHO MARRIED JACKIE AND MET AN UNTIMELY DEATH IN DALLAS, ONLY TO HAVE A NEW YORK AIRPORT NAMED AFTER HIM...... OH FOR GOD'S SAKE! NEXT QUESTION...
HIGH SCHOOL
DROPOUT BOWL
JOHN GRIMES

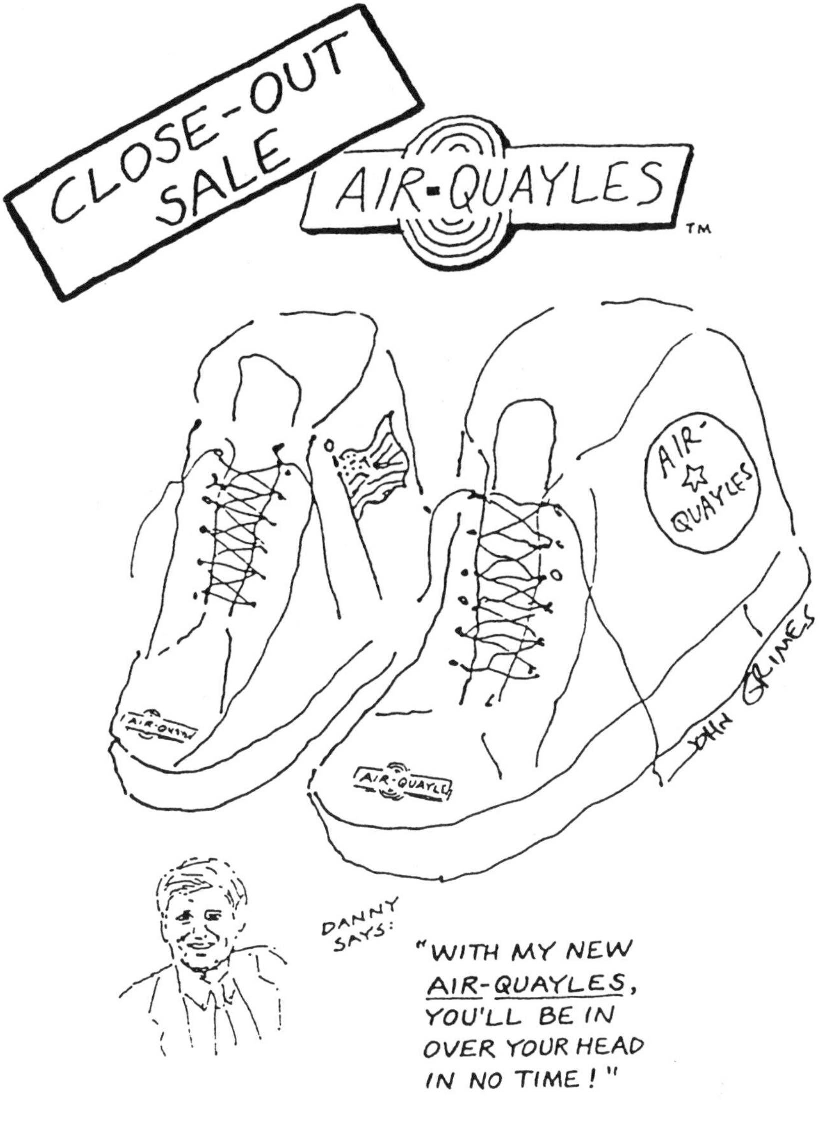
CLOSE-OUT SALE
AIR-QUAYLES ™
AIR- ☆ QUAYLES
DANNY SAYS:
"WITH MY NEW AIR-QUAYLES, YOU'LL BE IN OVER YOUR HEAD IN NO TIME!"

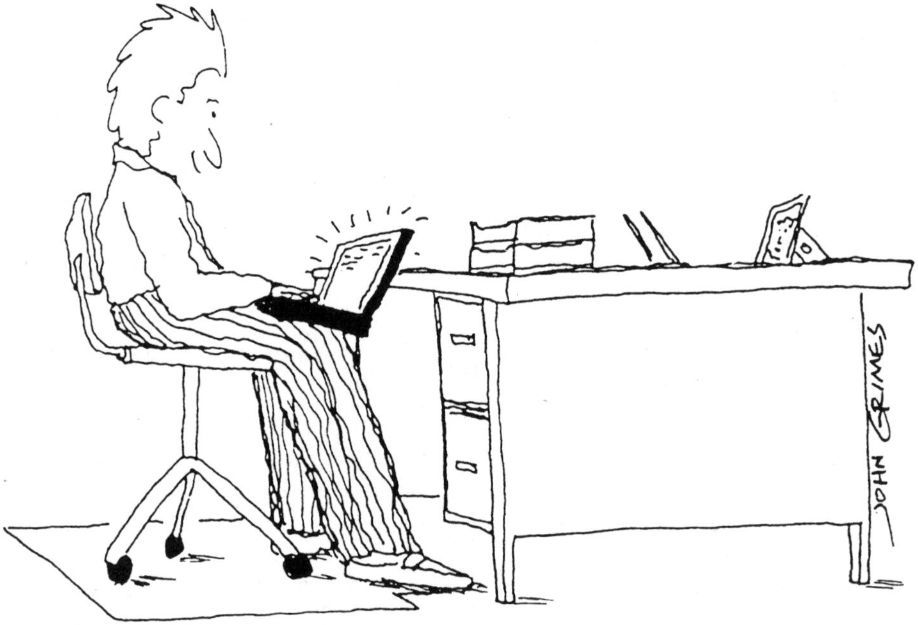
JOHN GRIMES

BOB LOVED HIS LAPTOP
BUT FOUND HIS DESK
OFTEN GOT IN THE WAY.

SCIENTISTS IN UTAH HAVE APPARENTLY RESOLVED MAN'S OLDEST DILEMMA...

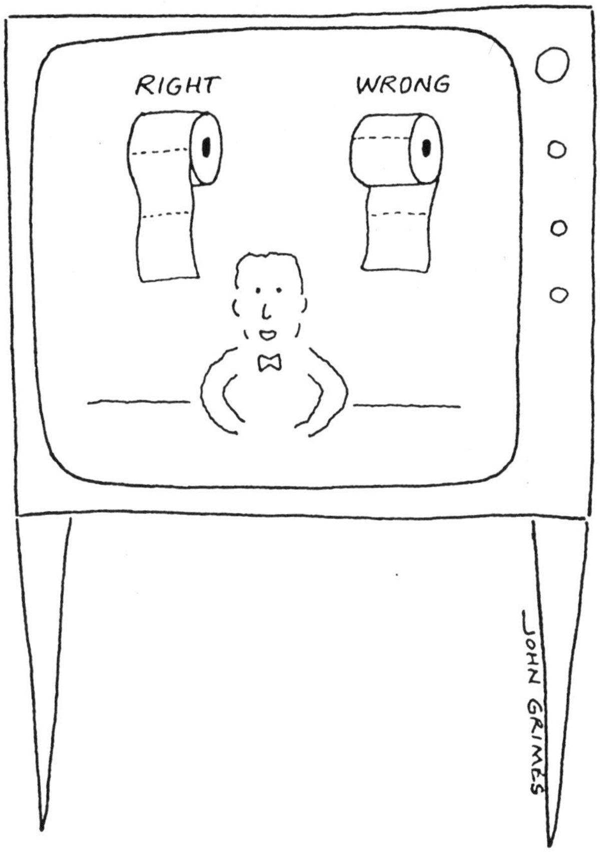
RIGHT
WRONG
JOHN GRIMES

MOOD FOR SEX
MOOD FOR SPORTS
JOHN GRIMES

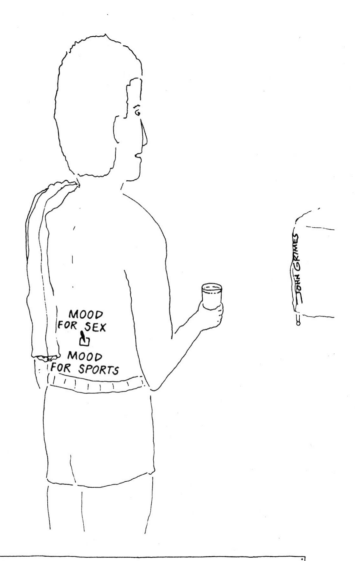

FEW WOMEN ARE AWARE
THAT MEN HAVE A TOGGLE SWITCH

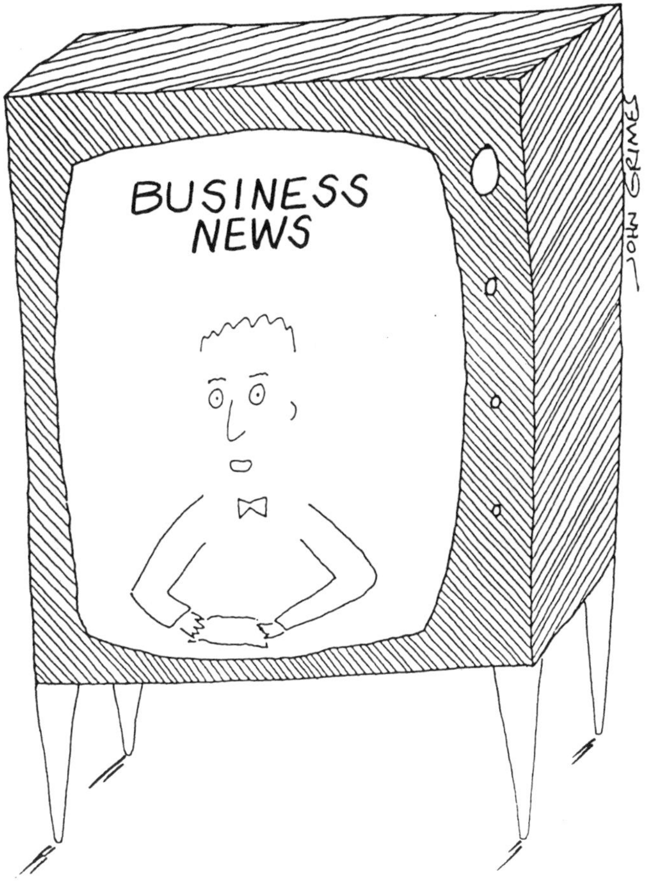
BUSINESS
NEWS
JOHN GRIMES

"TODAY THE FEDS ELIMINATED THE ECONOMIC INDEX FOR DURABLE GOODS. APPARENTLY NONE ARE PRODUCED ANYMORE."

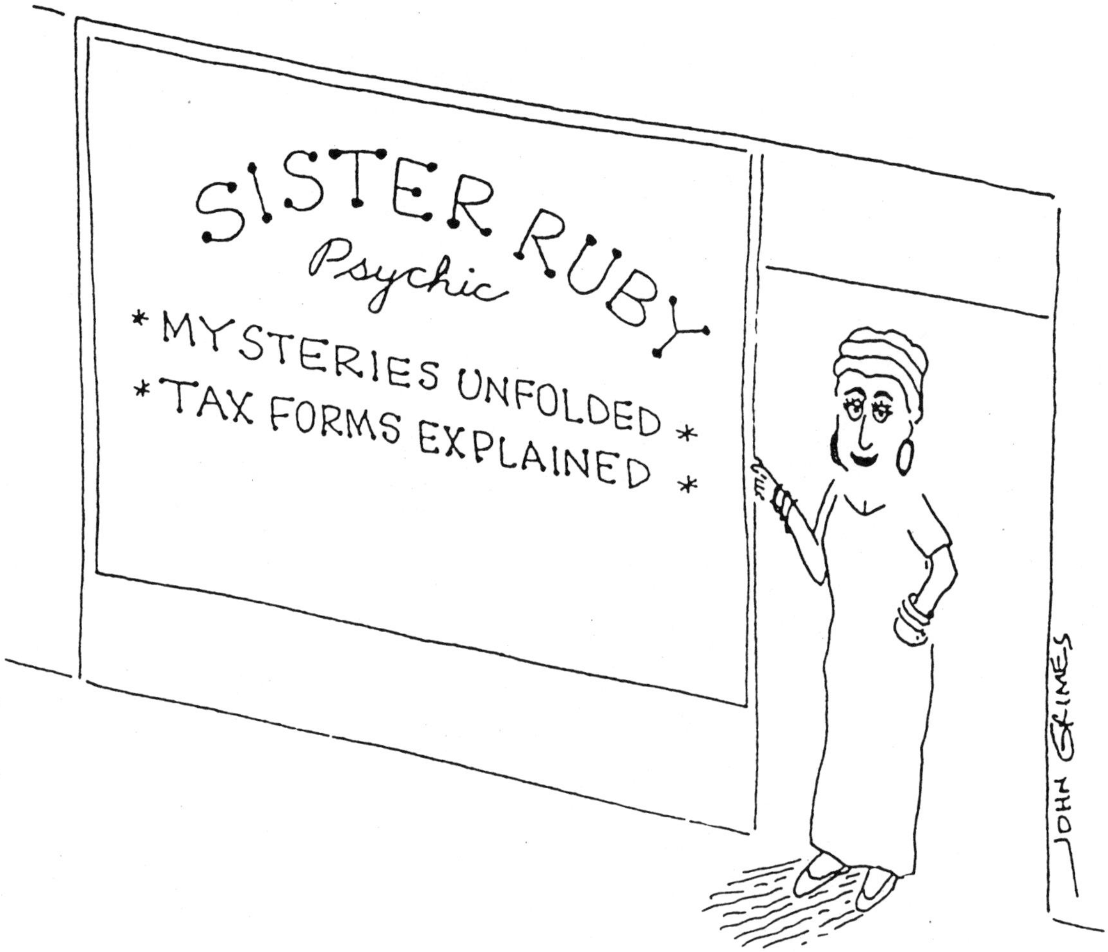
SISTER RUBY
Psychic
MYSTERIES UNFOLDED
TAX FORMS EXPLAINED
JOHN GRIMES

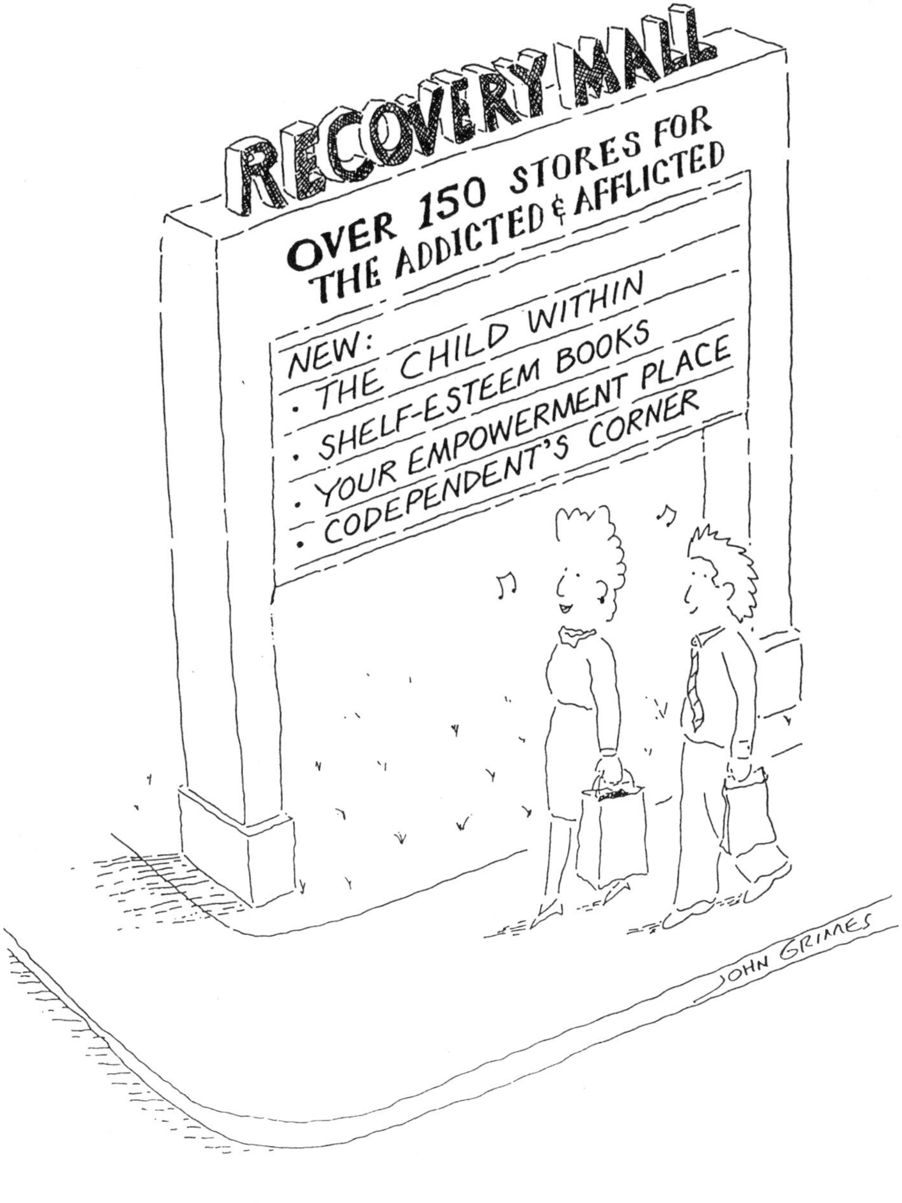
RECOVERY MALL
OVER 150 STORES FOR THE ADDICTED & AFFLICTED
NEW:
· THE CHILD WITHIN
· SHELF-ESTEEM BOOKS
· YOUR EMPOWERMENT PLACE
· CODEPENDENT'S CORNER
JOHN GRIMES

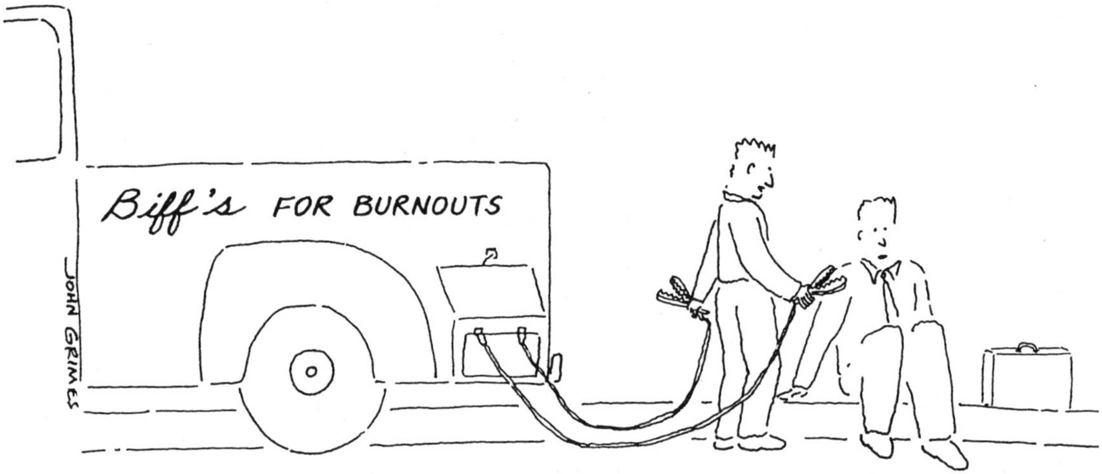
Biff's FOR BURNOUTS
JOHN GRIMES

SOMETIMES BOB NEEDED A JUMP START.

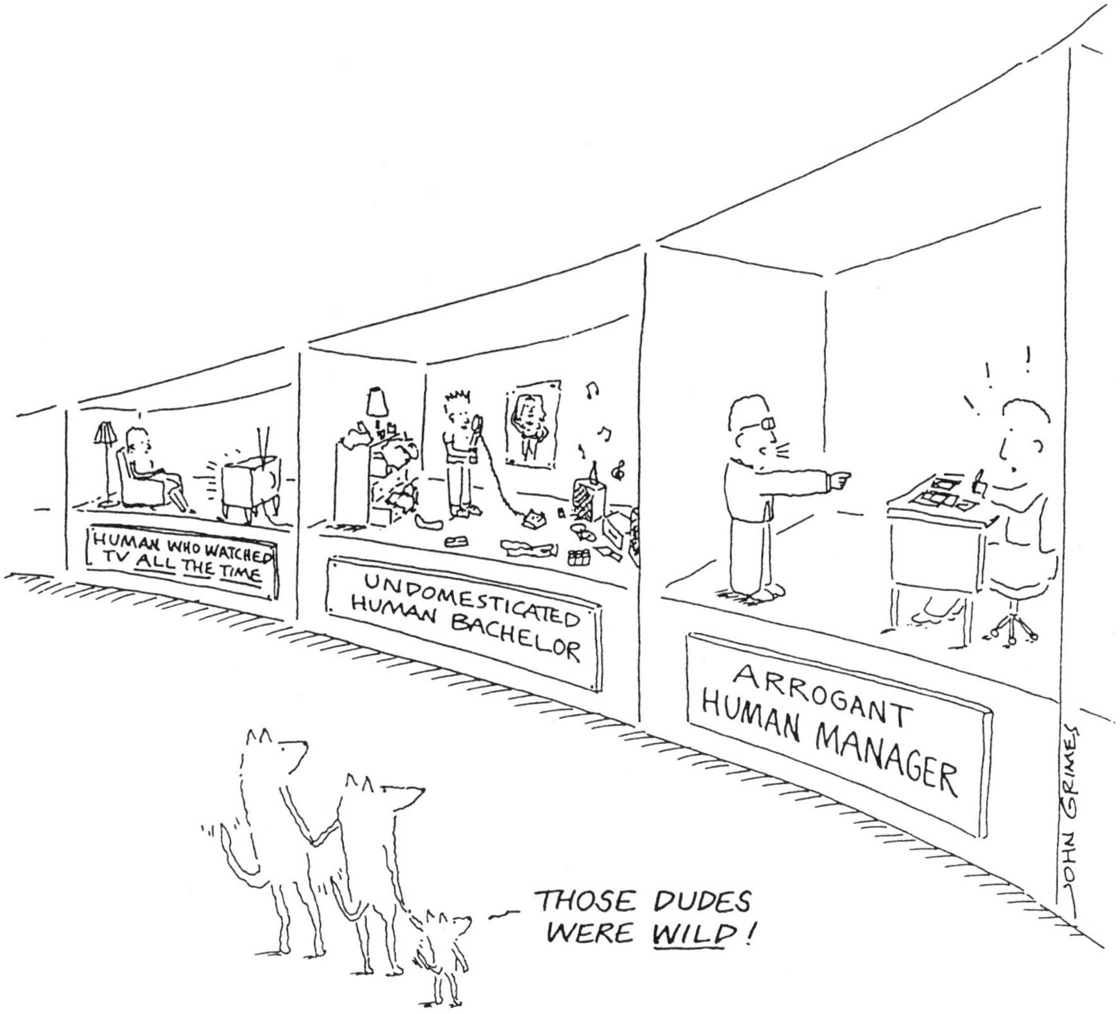
HUMAN WHO WATCHED TV ALL THE TIME
UNDOMESTICATED HUMAN BACHELOR
ARROGANT HUMAN MANAGER
JOHN GRIMES
THOSE DUDES WERE WILD!

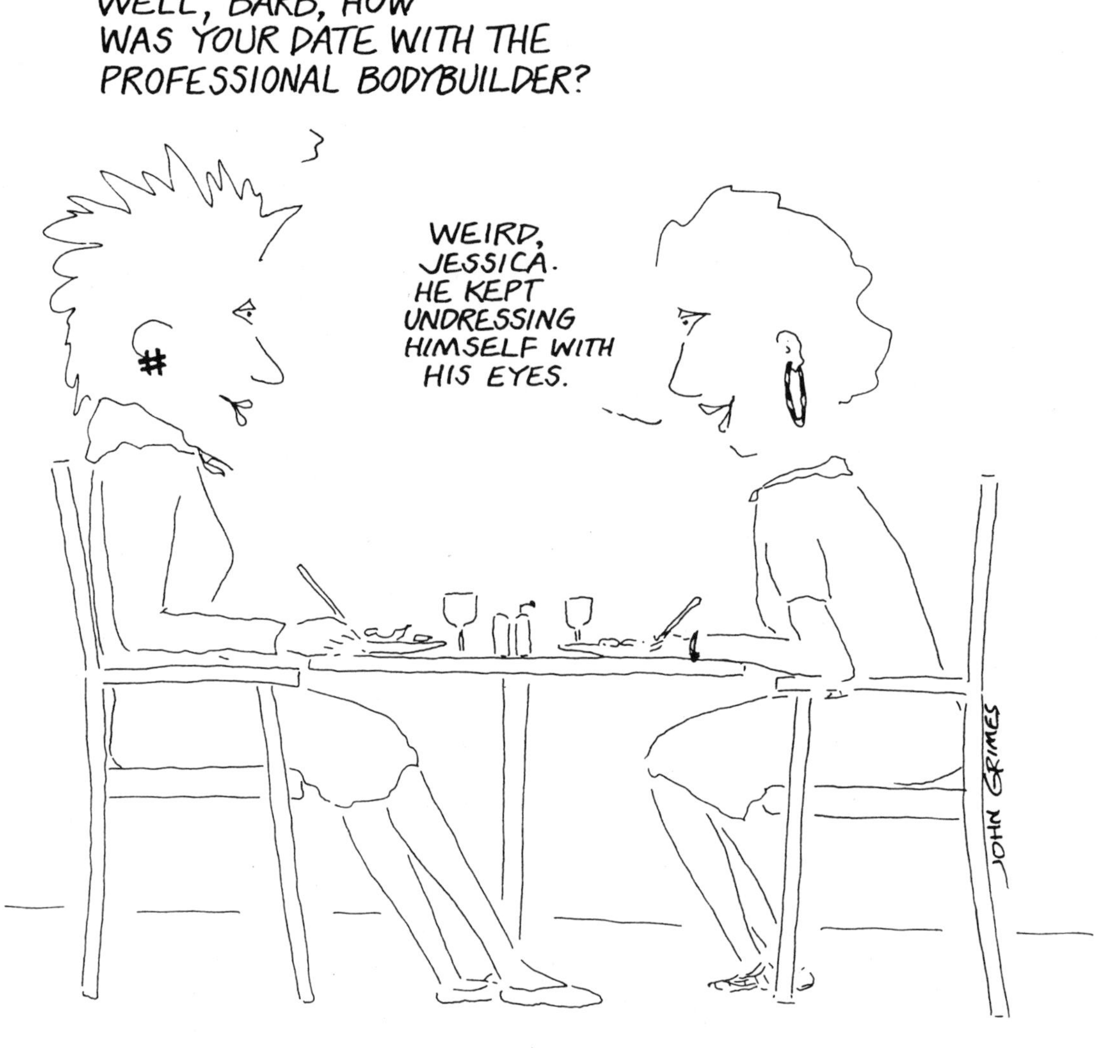
WELL, BARB, HOW WAS YOUR DATE WITH THE PROFESSIONAL BODYBUILDER?
WEIRD, JESSICA. HE KEPT UNDRESSING HIMSELF WITH HIS EYES.
JOHN GRIMES

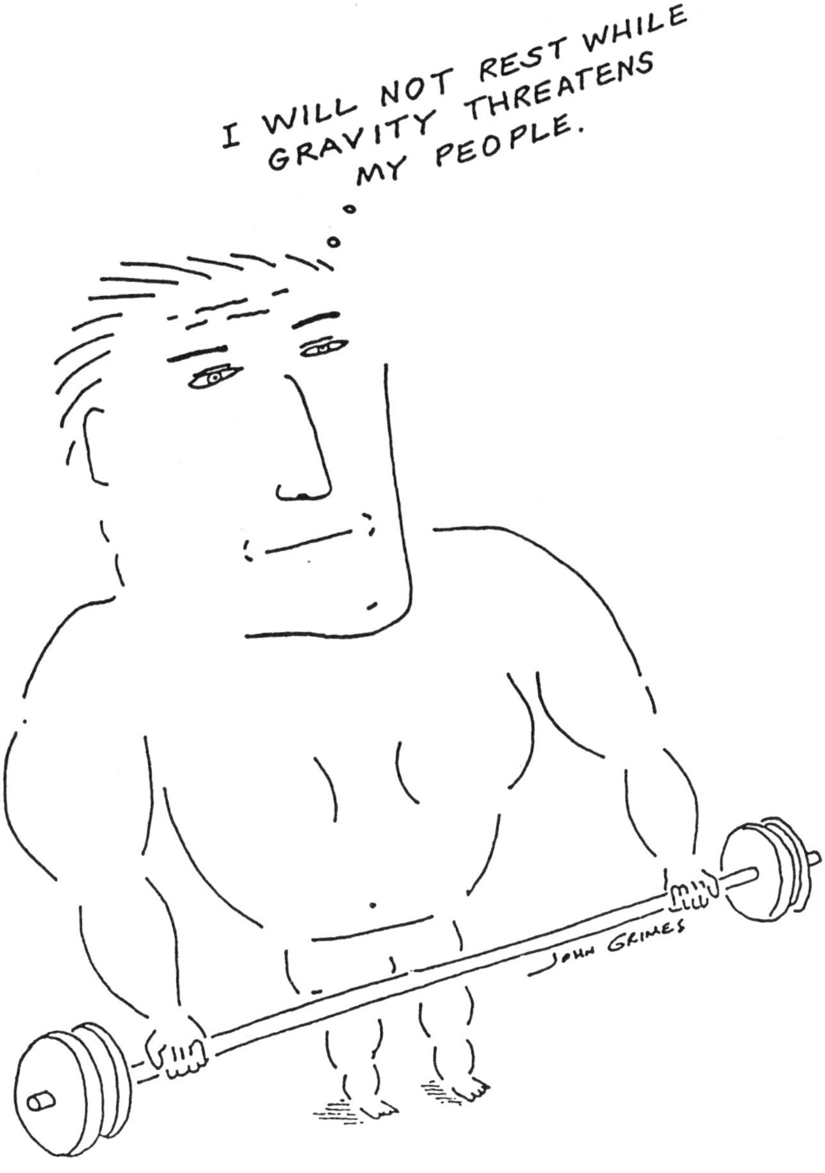
I WILL NOT REST WHILE GRAVITY THREATENS MY PEOPLE.
JOHN GRIMES

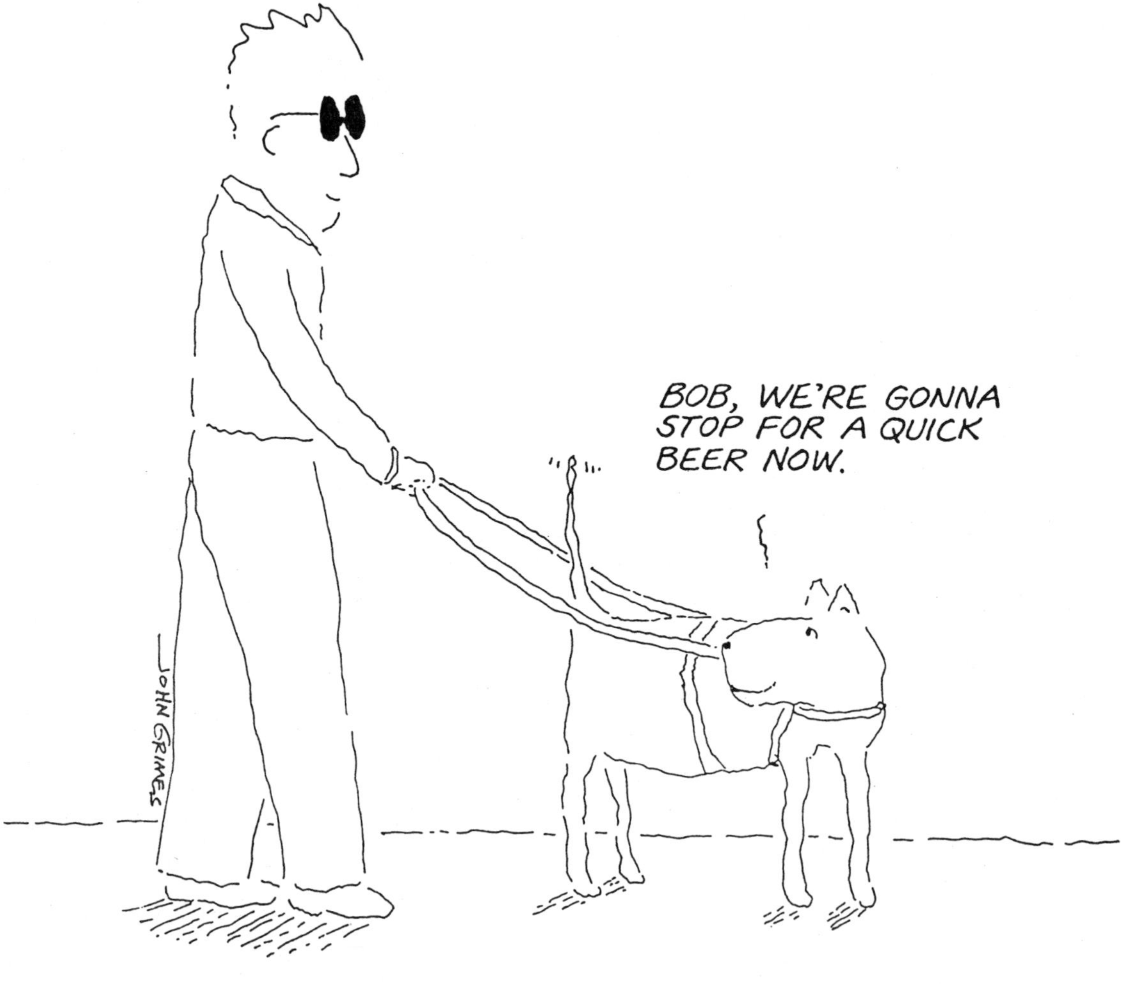
BOB, WE'RE GONNA STOP FOR A QUICK BEER NOW.
JOHN GRIMES

GUY DOG FOR THE BLIND

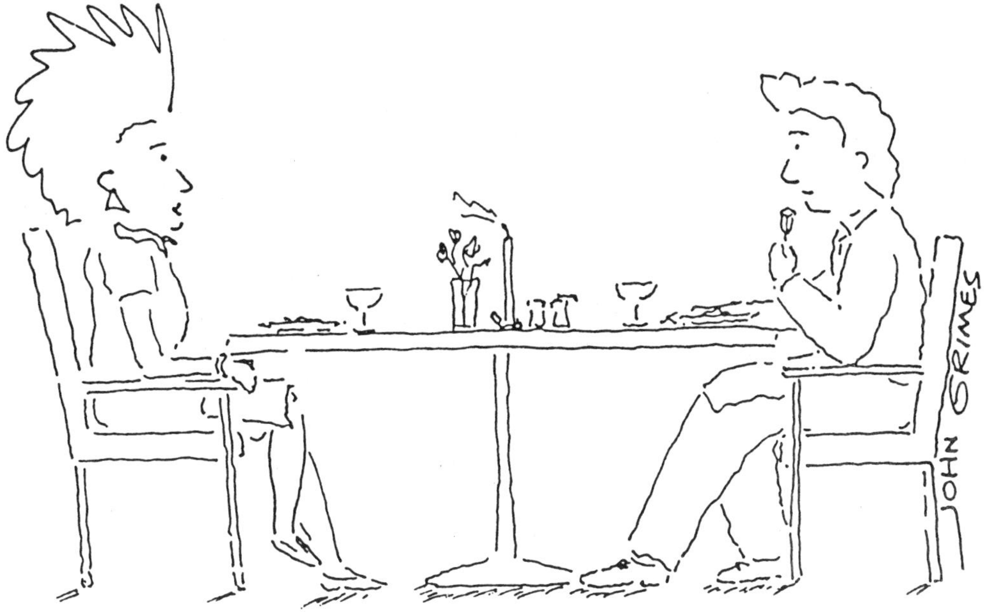
JOHN GRIMES

"BOB, I NEED MORE THAN SMALL TALK. I NEED LARGE TALK."

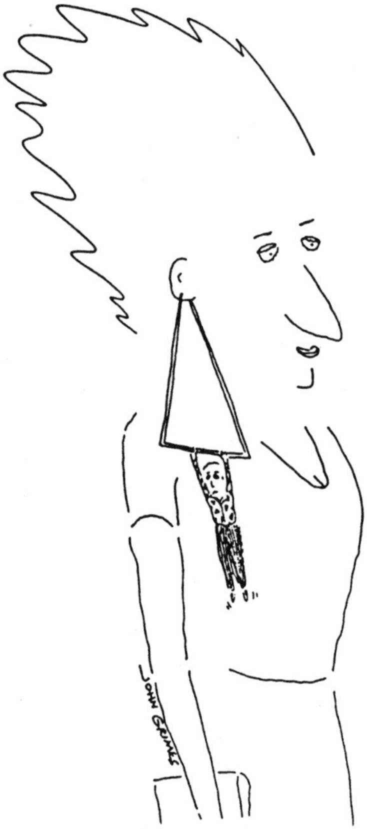
JOHN GRIMES

At first, Dwayne's gymnastic prowess had mesmerized Sarah, but now she longed for more than he could ever deliver. Yet Dwayne clung desparately, on one level disillusioned with powerful women, on another level looking forward to falling out of love and onto the soft carpet below.

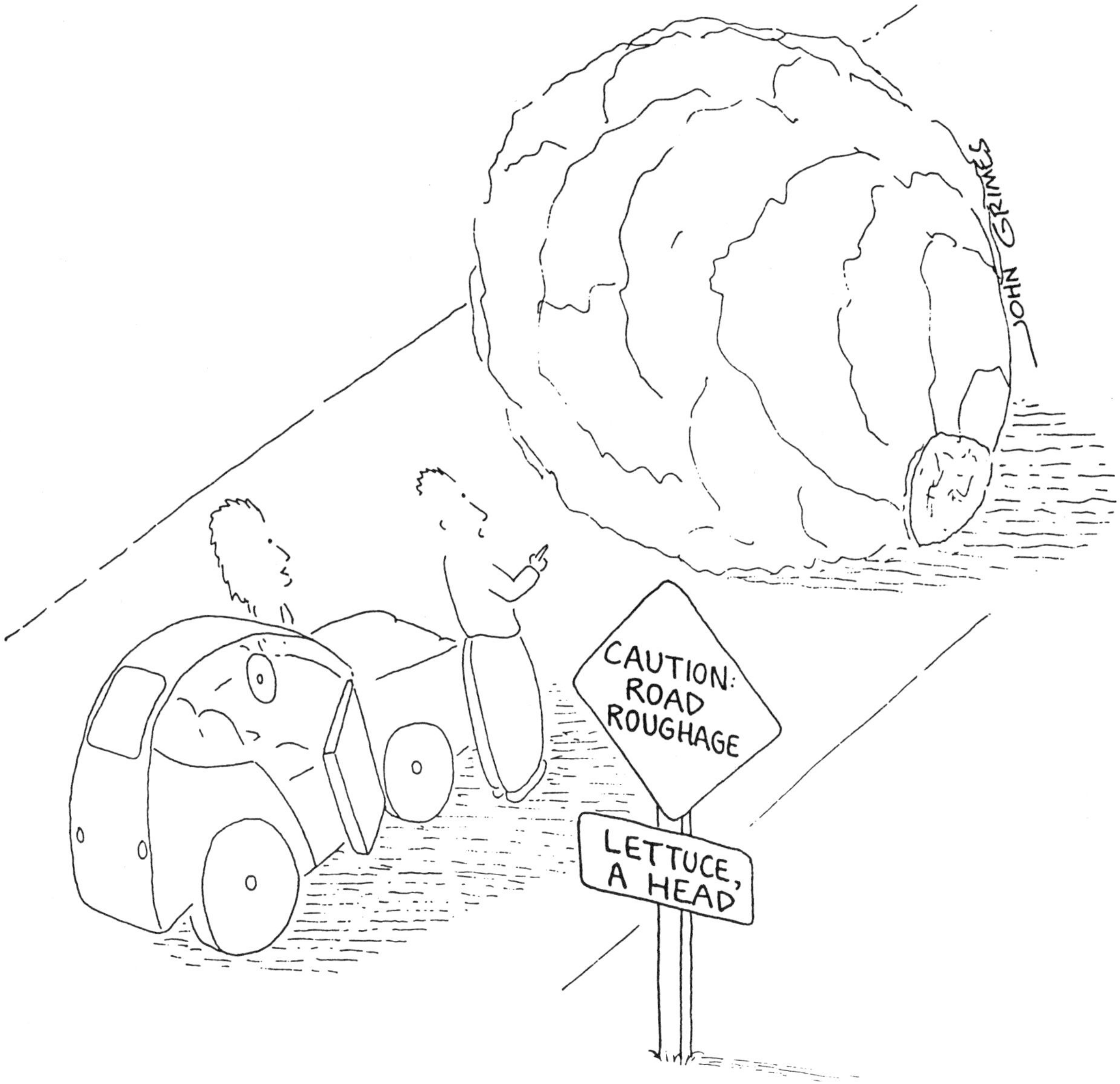
CAUTION:
ROAD
ROUGHAGE
LETTUCE,
A HEAD
JOHN GRIMES

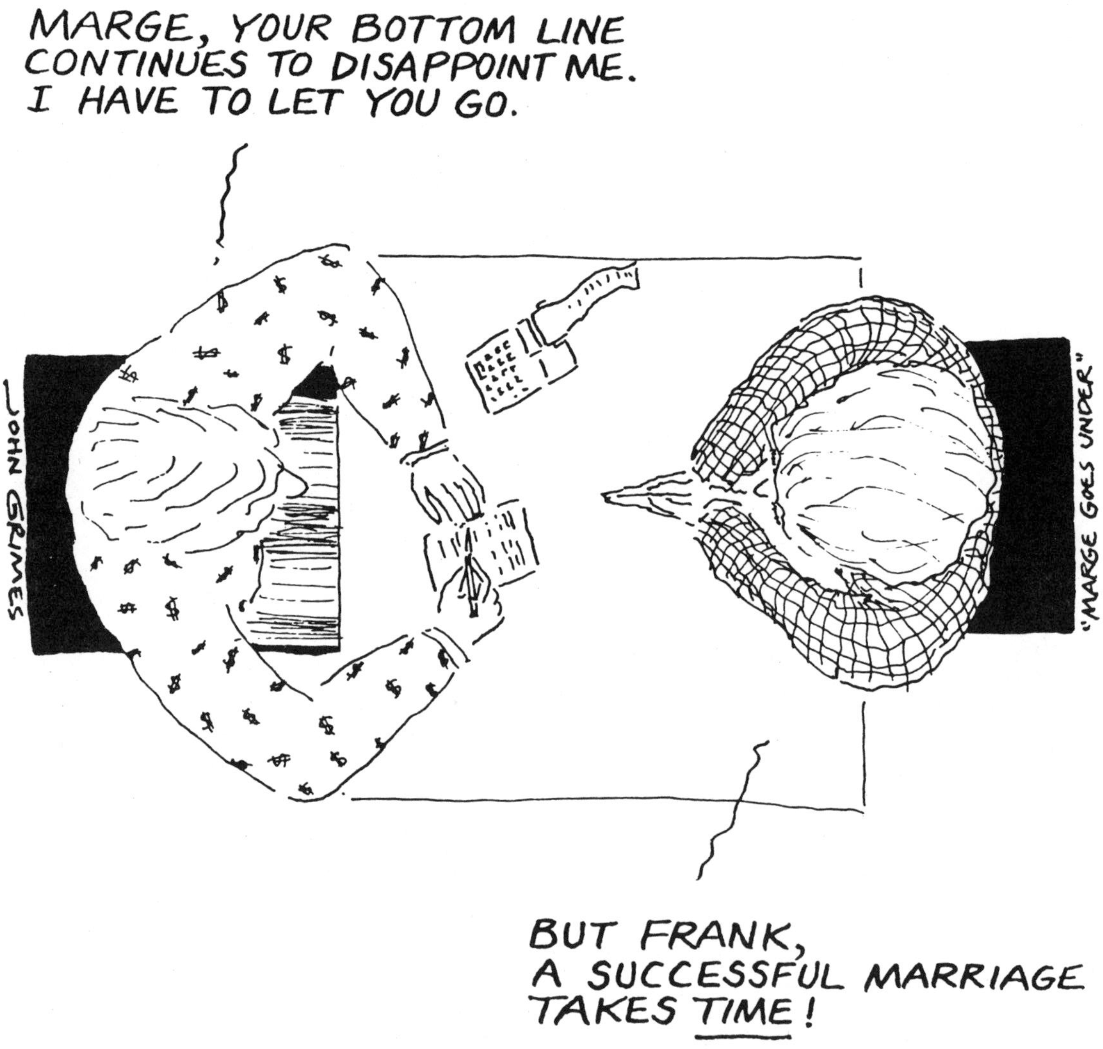
MARGE, YOUR BOTTOM LINE CONTINUES TO DISAPPOINT ME. I HAVE TO LET YOU GO.
BUT FRANK, A SUCCESSFUL MARRIAGE TAKES TIME!
JOHN GRIMES
"MARGE GOES UNDER"

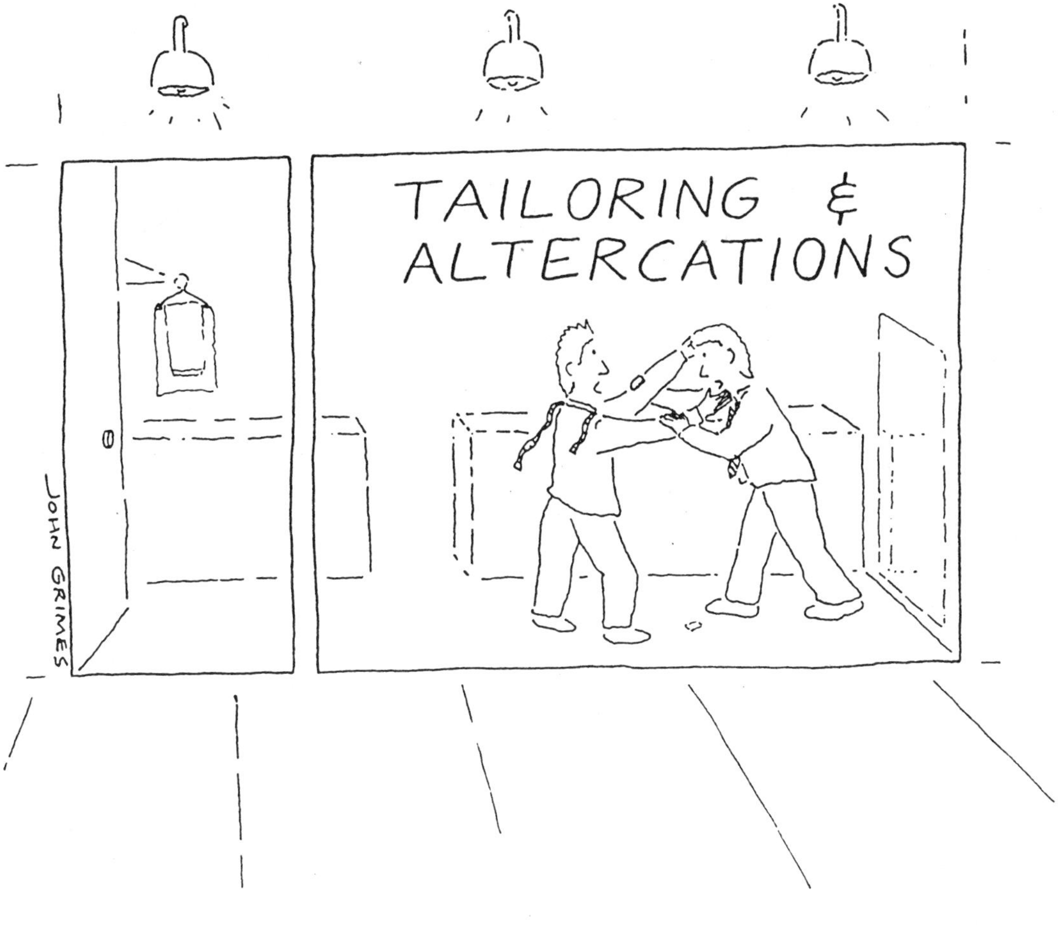
TAILORING &
ALTERCATIONS
JOHN GRIMES

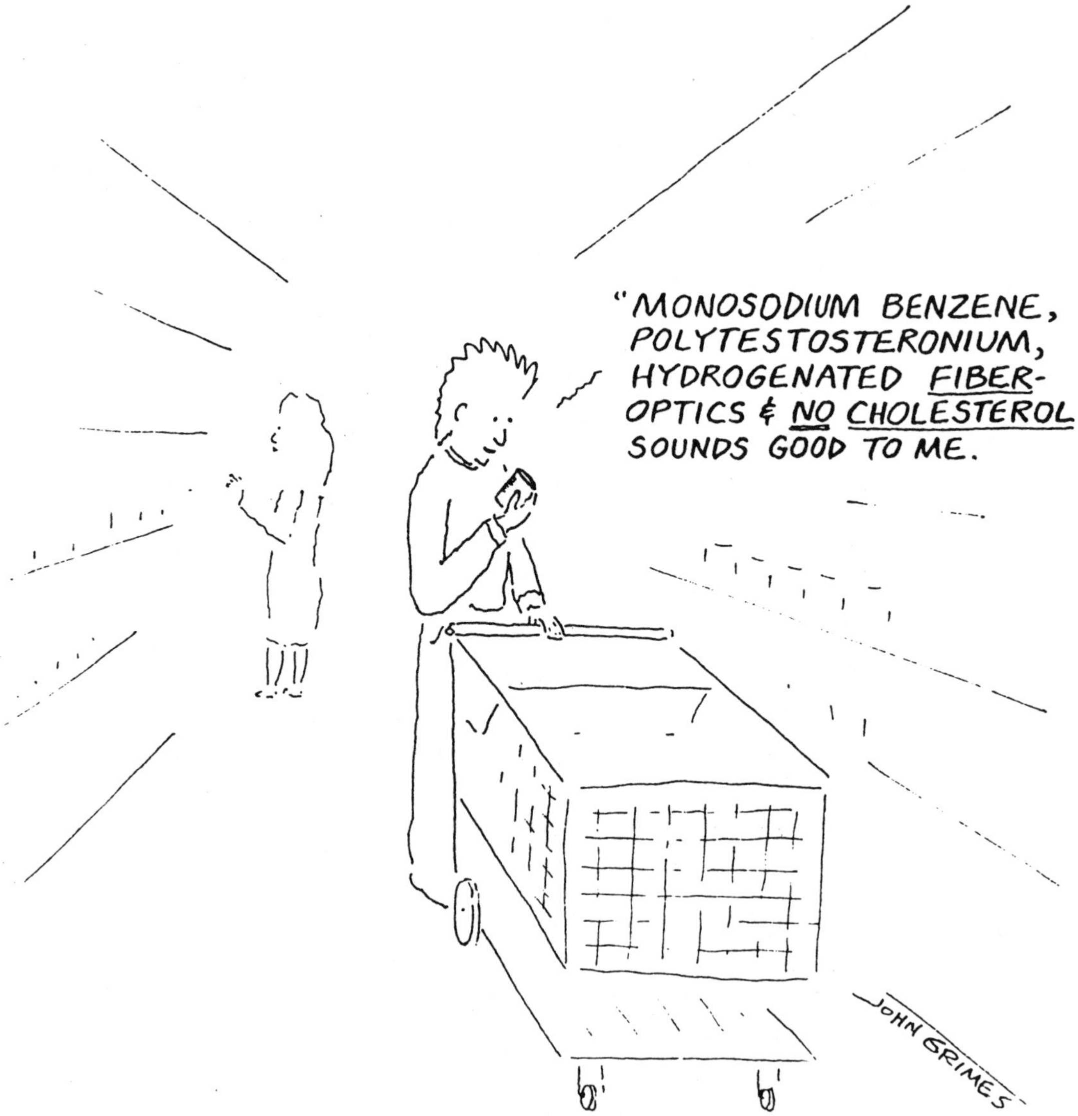
"MONOSODIUM BENZENE, POLYTESTOSTERONIUM, HYDROGENATED FIBER-OPTICS & NO CHOLESTEROL!" SOUNDS GOOD TO ME.
JOHN GRIMES

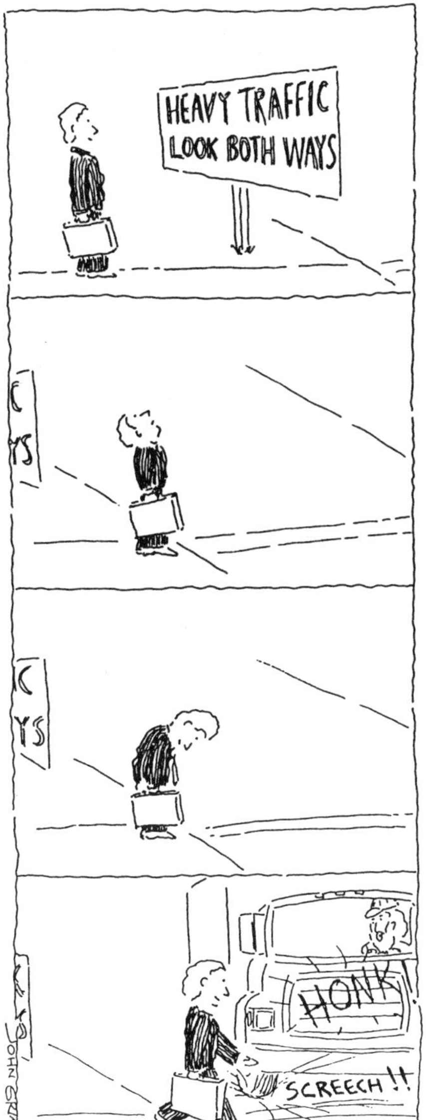
HEAVY TRAFFIC
LOOK BOTH WAYS
HONK!!
SCREECH!!
JOHN GRIMES

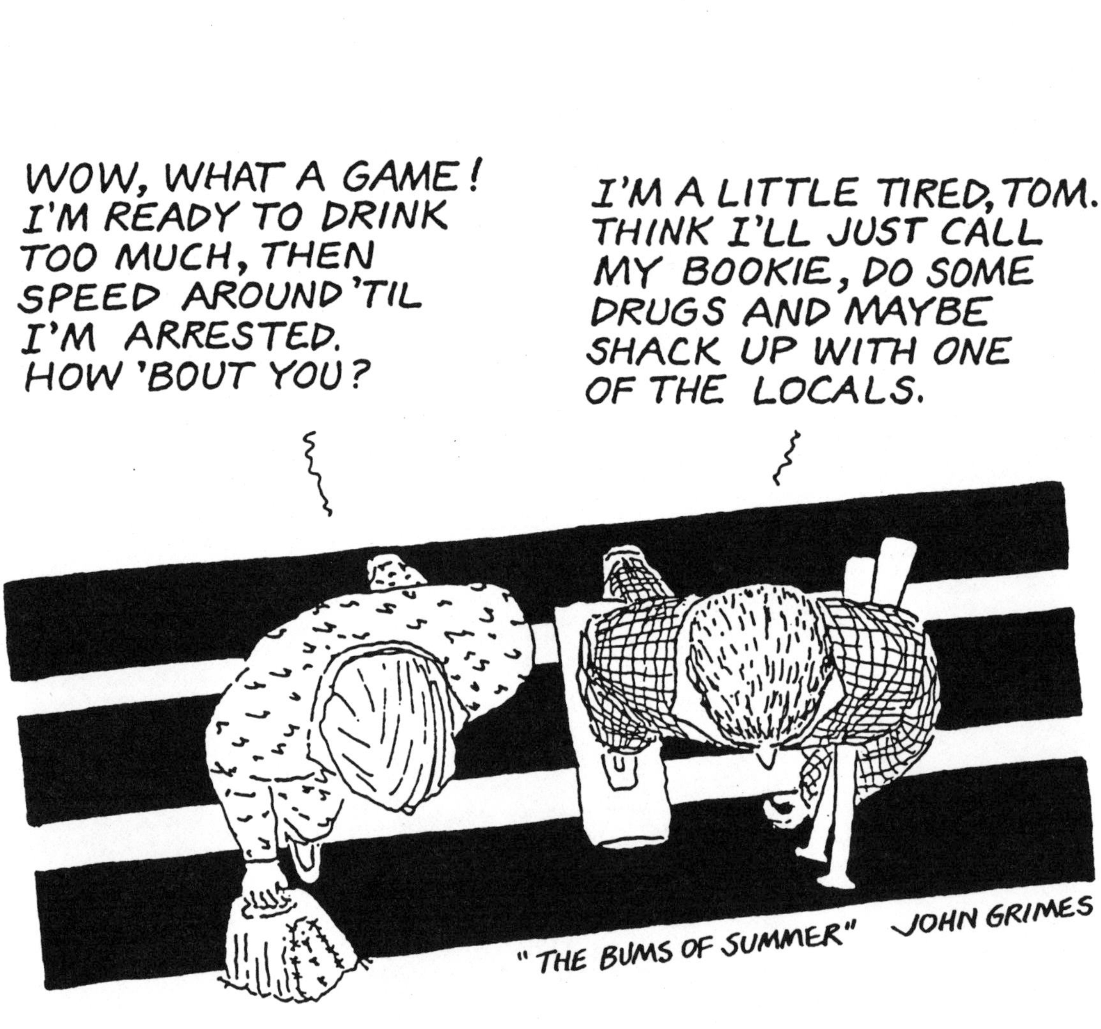
WOW, WHAT A GAME! I'M READY TO DRINK TOO MUCH, THEN SPEED AROUND 'TIL I'M ARRESTED. HOW 'BOUT YOU?
I'M A LITTLE TIRED, TOM. THINK I'LL JUST CALL MY BOOKIE, DO SOME DRUGS AND MAYBE SHACK UP WITH ONE OF THE LOCALS.
"THE BUMS OF SUMMER" JOHN GRIMES

DOC, I'M LOSING MY AGGRESSIVENESS. SOMETIMES I'M EVEN SENSITIVE TO THE NEEDS OF OTHERS.
IT'S YOUR MASCULINITY SYSTEM, SAM — JUST ABOUT SHOT... HEY! HAVE YOU BEEN WATCHING OPRAH?
EXIT
JOHN GRIMES

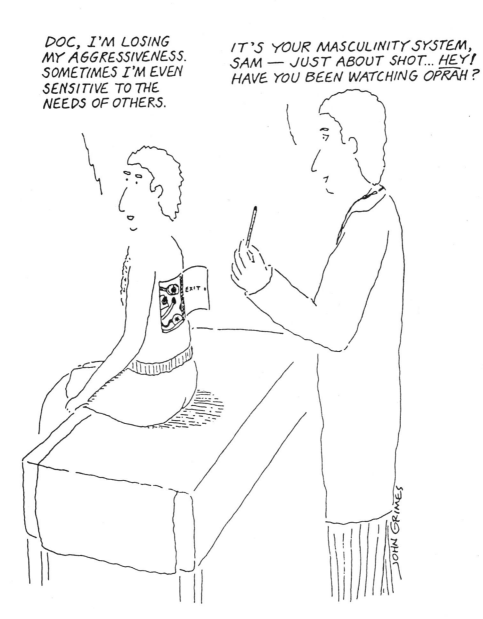

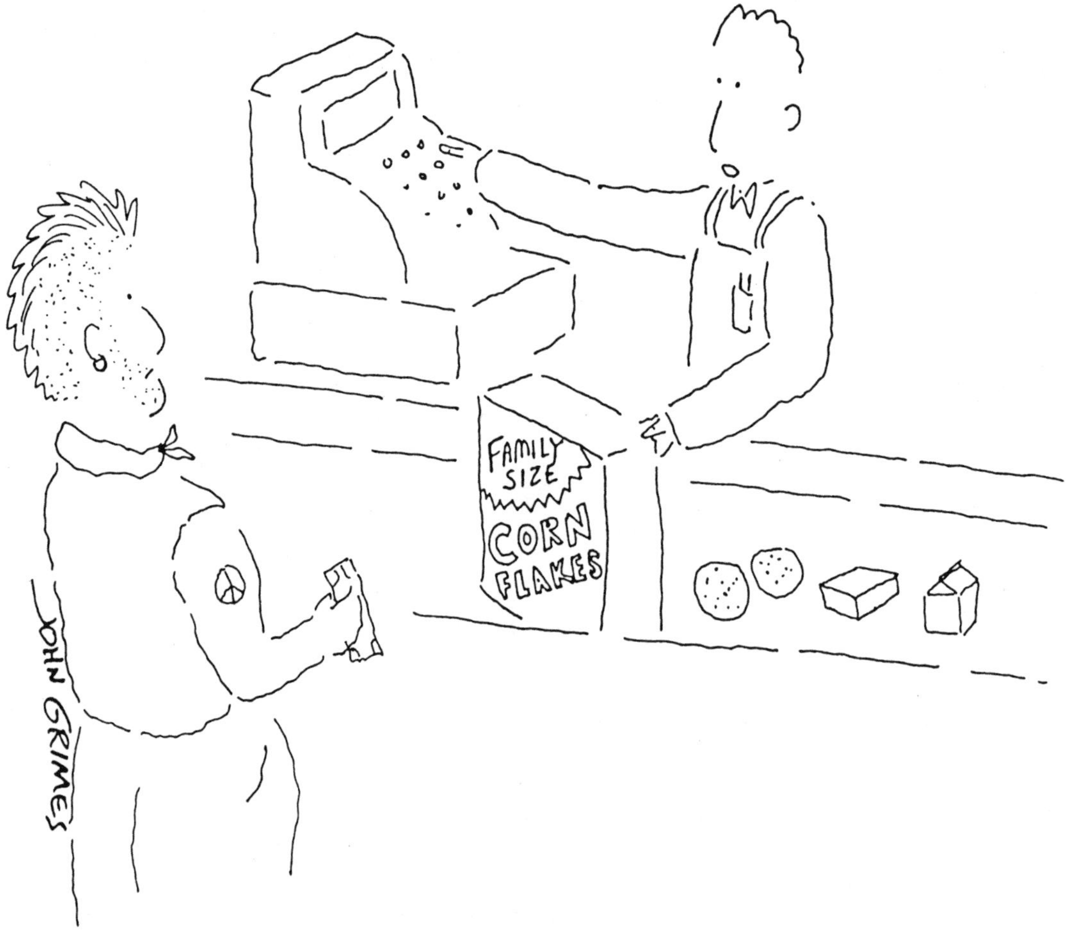
FAMILY SIZE
CORN FLAKES
JOHN GRIMES

"SORRY SIR, I'LL NEED TO SEE PROOF OF FAMILY VALUES."

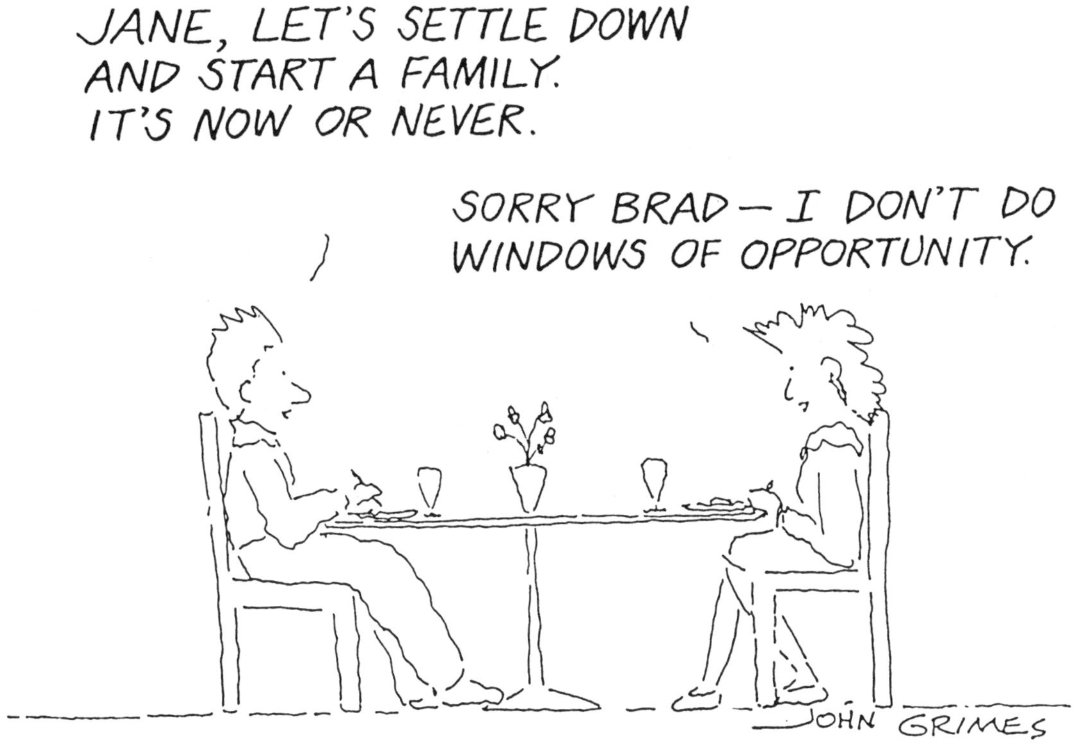
JANE, LET'S SETTLE DOWN AND START A FAMILY. IT'S NOW OR NEVER.
SORRY BRAD — I DON'T DO WINDOWS OF OPPORTUNITY.
JOHN GRIMES

♪ *♪*

"RING AROUND THE WALLET, RING AROUND THE WALLET"

SO TACKY!

WHY SUFFER THE EMBARRASSMENT OF UNSIGHTLY "RUBBER-RING?"

JUST LOOK AT HOW HAMBLY'S NEW "CONDOMIZER"™ BILLFOLD HIDES YOUR LITTLE FRIEND:

SO CHIC!

ALSO AVAILABLE: "CONDOMIZER"™ BRIEFCASES, PURSES & STEAMER TRUNKS FOR YOU HEAVY USERS!

JOHN GRIMES

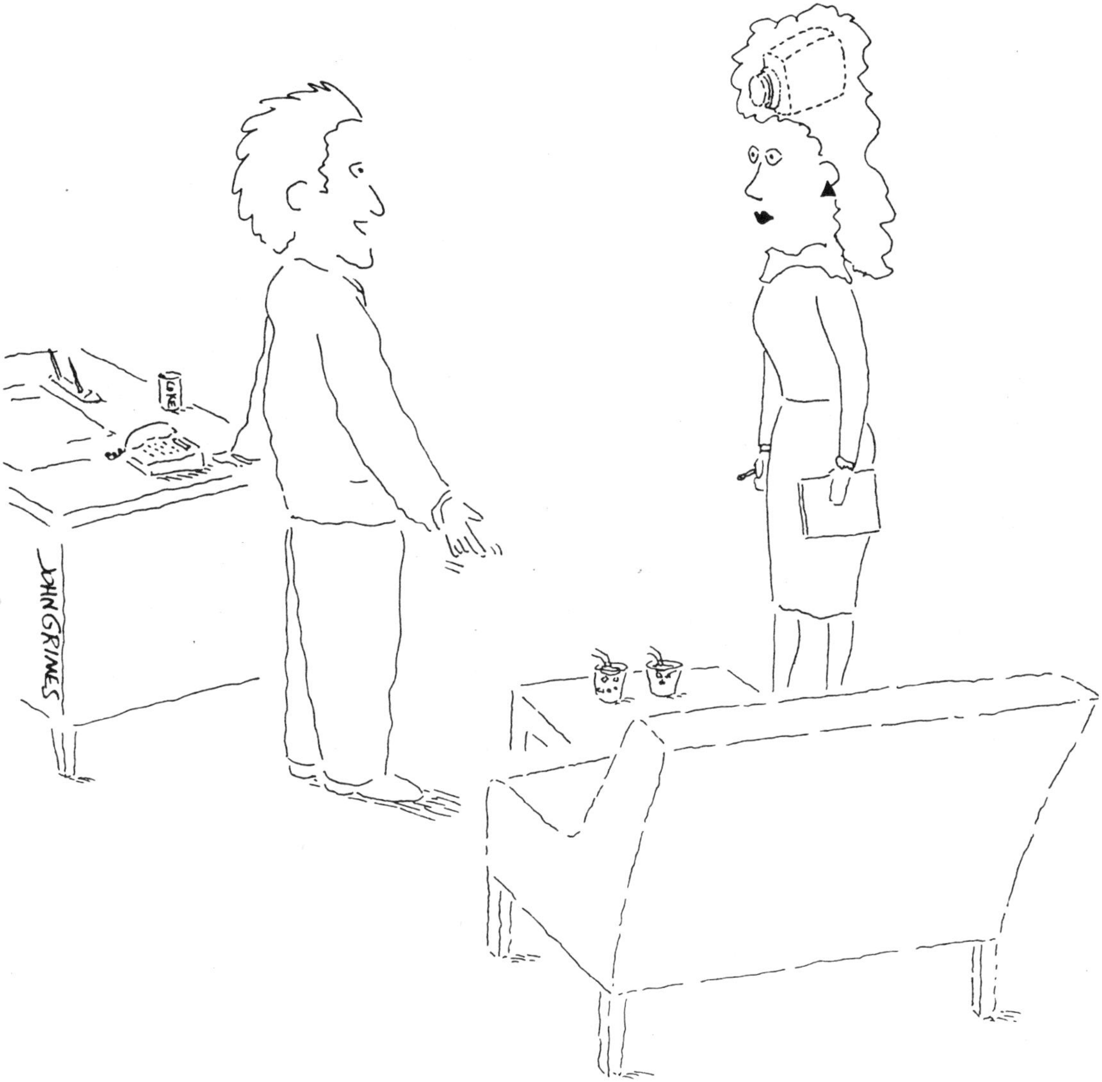
JOHN GRIMES

BETSY SENSED THAT HER NEWLY-INSTALLED "ANITA HILL COIF-CAM" WOULD BE COMING IN HANDY.

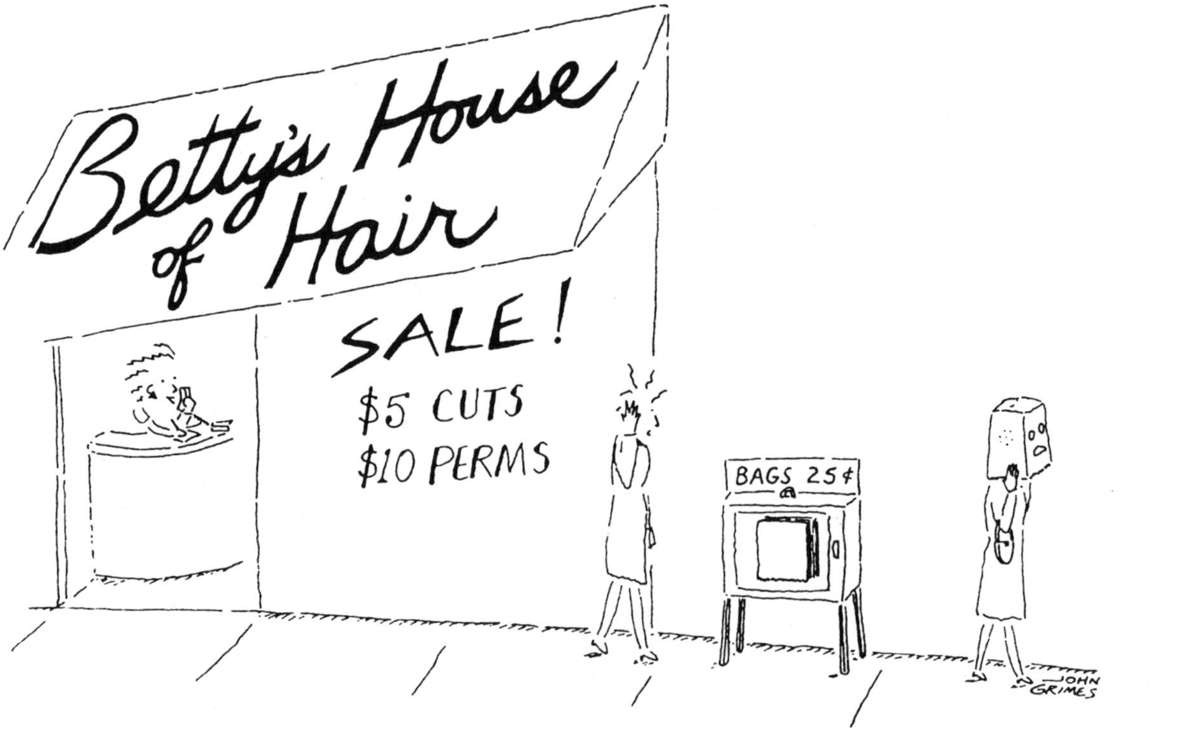

Betty's House of Hair
SALE!
$5 CUTS
$10 PERMS
BAGS 25¢
JOHN GRIMES

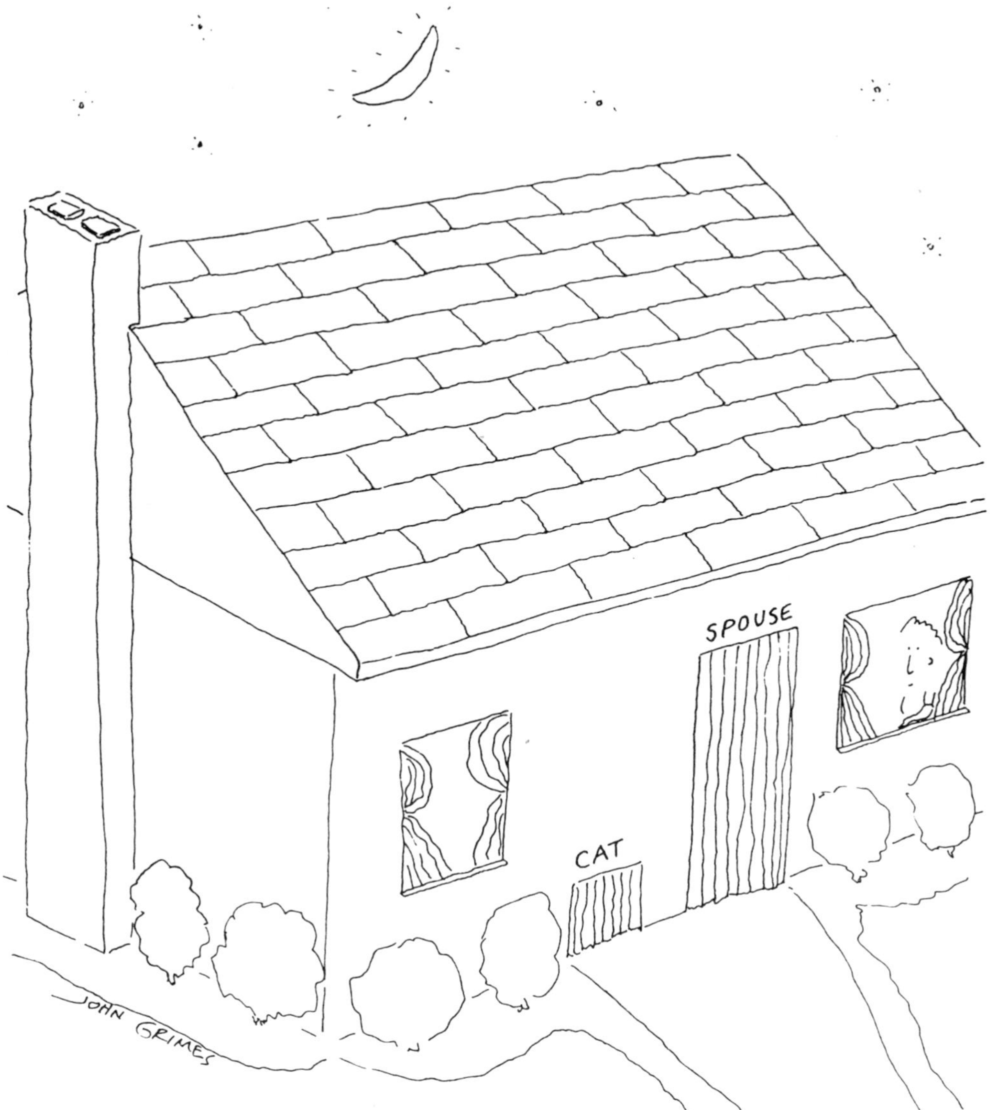
SPOUSE
CAT
JOHN GRIMES

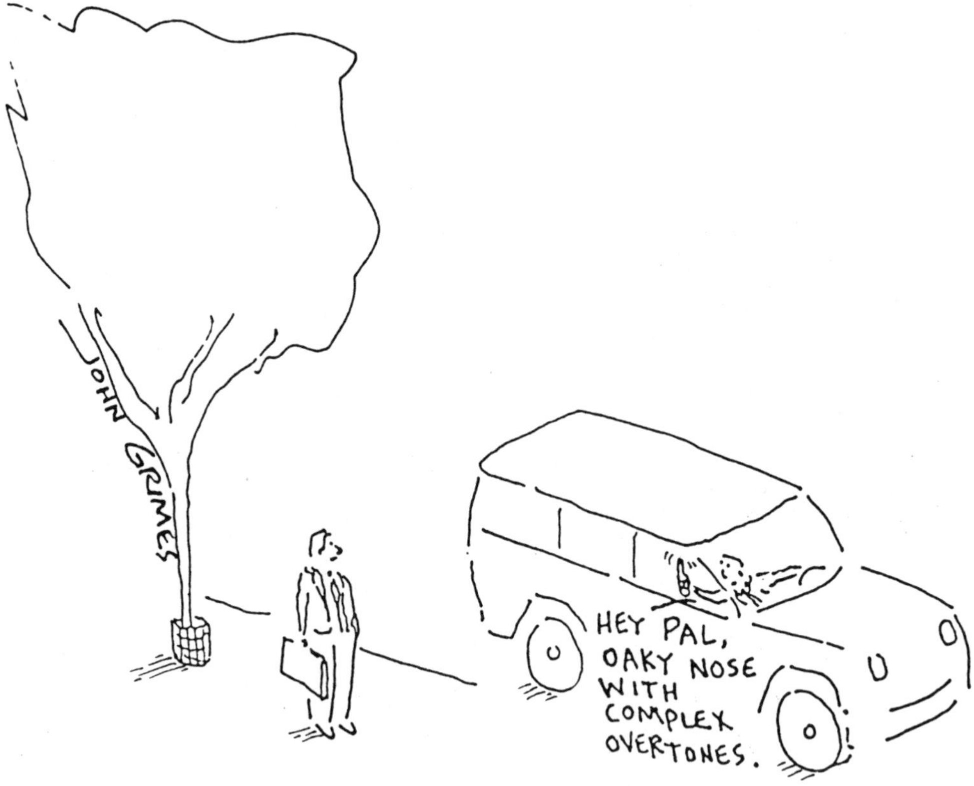
JOHN GRIMES
HEY PAL, OAKY NOSE WITH COMPLEX OVERTONES.

A NOTORIOUS CHARDONNAY DEALER CRUISES FOR CLIENTS

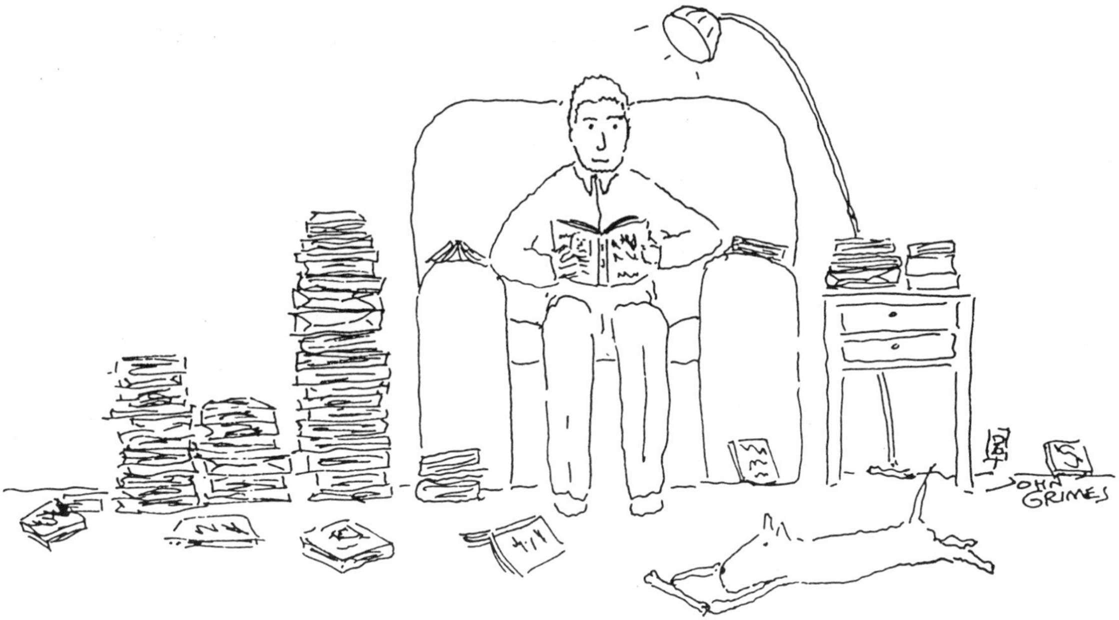
JOHN GRIMES

BARRY NOW HAD SECOND THOUGHTS ABOUT THE BOOK-OF-THE-DAY CLUB.

1
BEEP! BEEP!
2
HONEY, IT'S TIME TO MAKE LOVE!
JOHN GRIMES

BILL NEEDED TO WORK ON HIS SPONTANEITY.

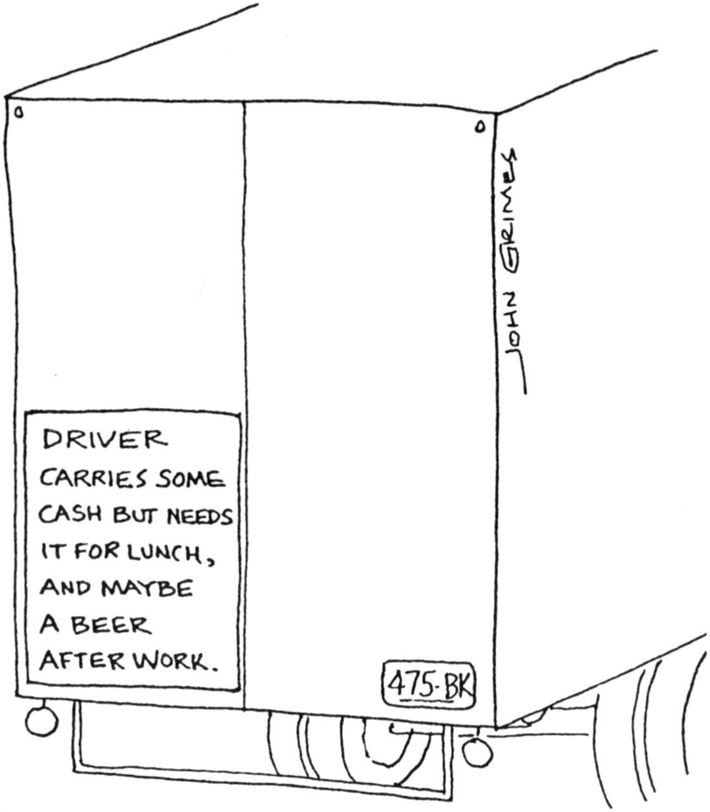

DRIVER
CARRIES SOME
CASH BUT NEEDS
IT FOR LUNCH,
AND MAYBE
A BEER
AFTER WORK.
475-BK
JOHN GRIMES

MAGAZINES OUR PARENTS USED TO READ
JUST WAIT TILL YOUR FATHER GETS HOME
MONTHLY
5¢
IF THERE'S ONE MORE PEEP OUT OF YOU!
REVIEW
SUMMER DISCIPLINE ISSUE
YOU'LL UNDERSTAND WHEN YOU'RE OLDER
J·O·U·R·N·A·L
???
Don't Stare at Grandma's Mustache
MAGAZINE
JOHN GRIMES

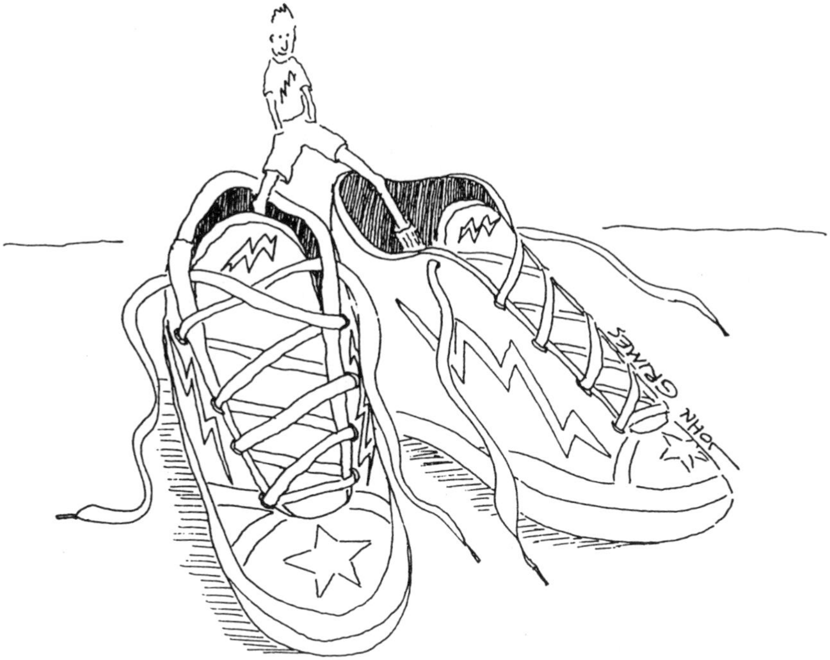
JOHN GRIMES

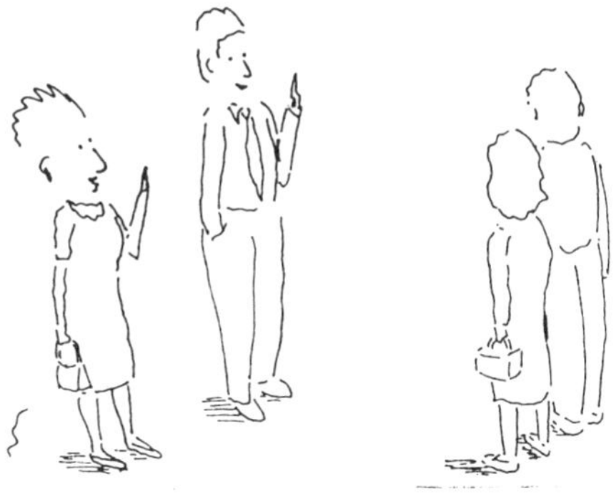

WE'D LIKE YOU TO MEET ROBBIE'S SHOES,
AND OF COURSE, ROBBIE HIMSELF.

OFFICE MUGS OF THE BOLD

LET'S SKIP OUT EARLY & GRAB A FEW DRINKS!

THIS COMPANY'S GOING NOWHERE!

JOHN GRIMES

WHY BUY PENS & PENCILS WHEN YOU CAN GET THEM FREE AT THE OFFICE?

MY BOSS IS A TWIT

IF YOU THINK THE COFFEE'S WEAK, YOU SHOULD SEE OUR ANNUAL REPORT!

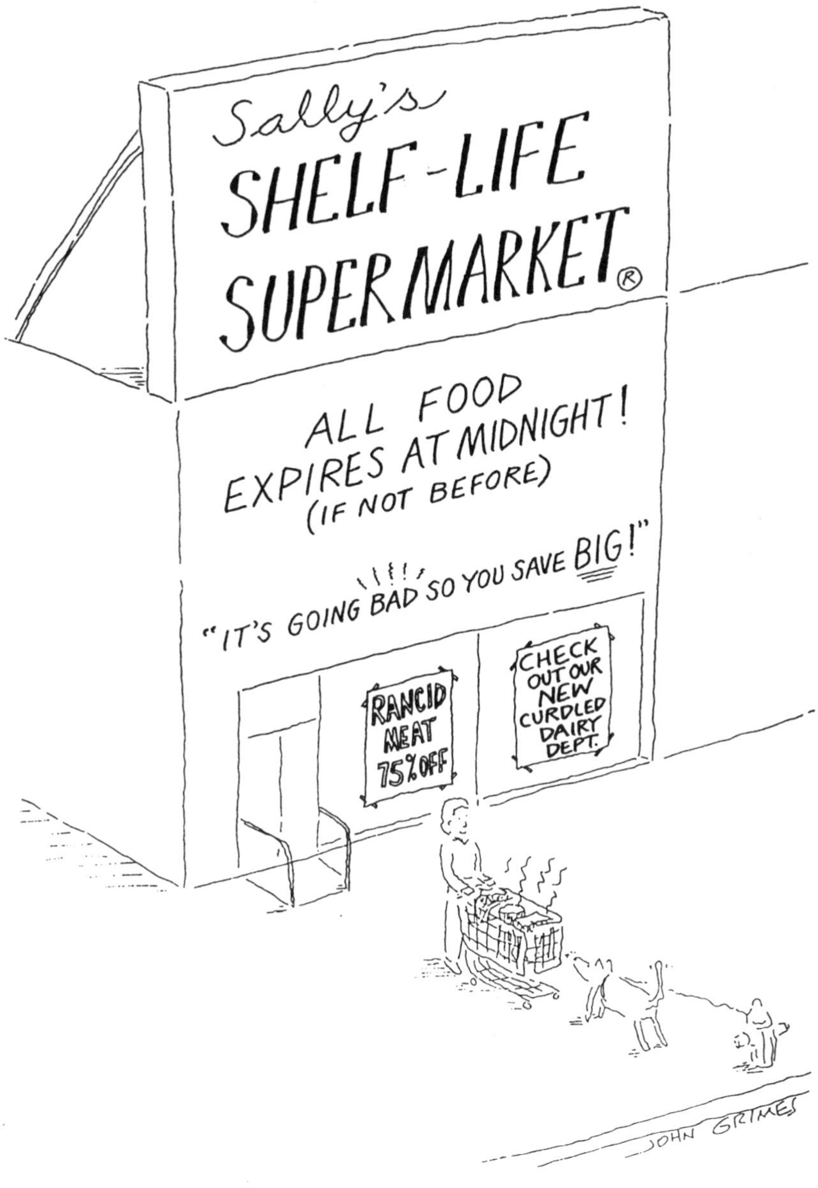
Sally's
SHELF-LIFE
SUPERMARKET®
ALL FOOD
EXPIRES AT MIDNIGHT!
(IF NOT BEFORE)
"IT'S GOING BAD SO YOU SAVE BIG!"
RANCID MEAT 75% OFF
CHECK OUT OUR NEW CURDLED DAIRY DEPT.
JOHN GRIMES

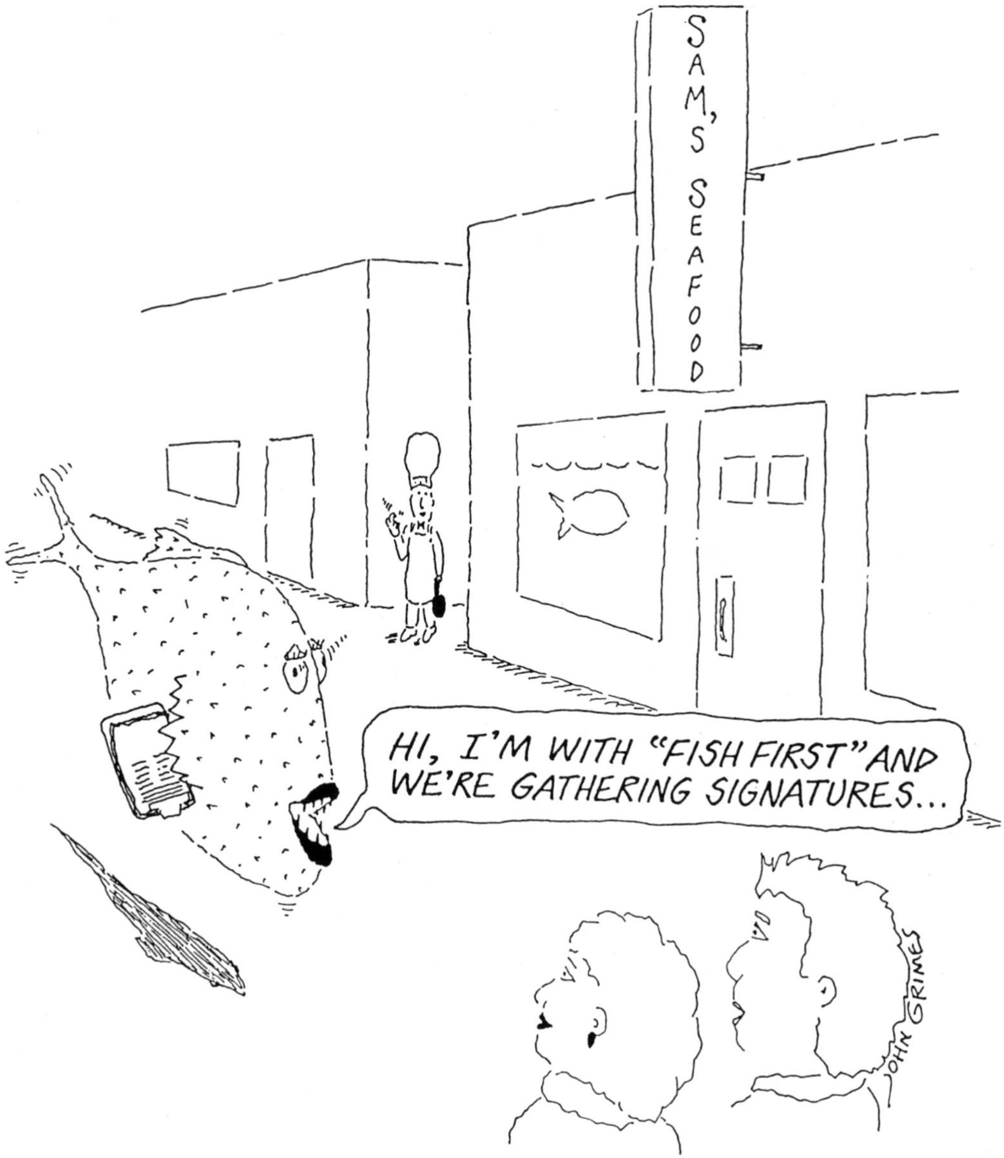
SAM'S SEAFOOD
HI, I'M WITH "FISH FIRST" AND WE'RE GATHERING SIGNATURES...
JOHN GRIMES

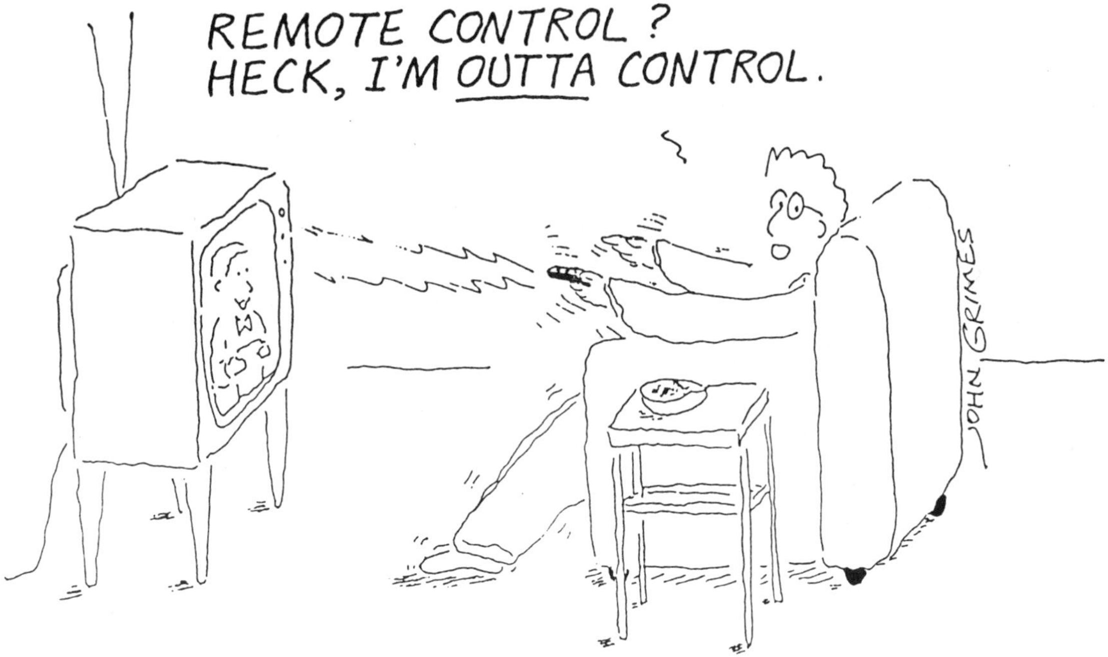
REMOTE CONTROL ?
HECK, I'M OUTTA CONTROL.
JOHN GRIMES

FRANK ZAPPER

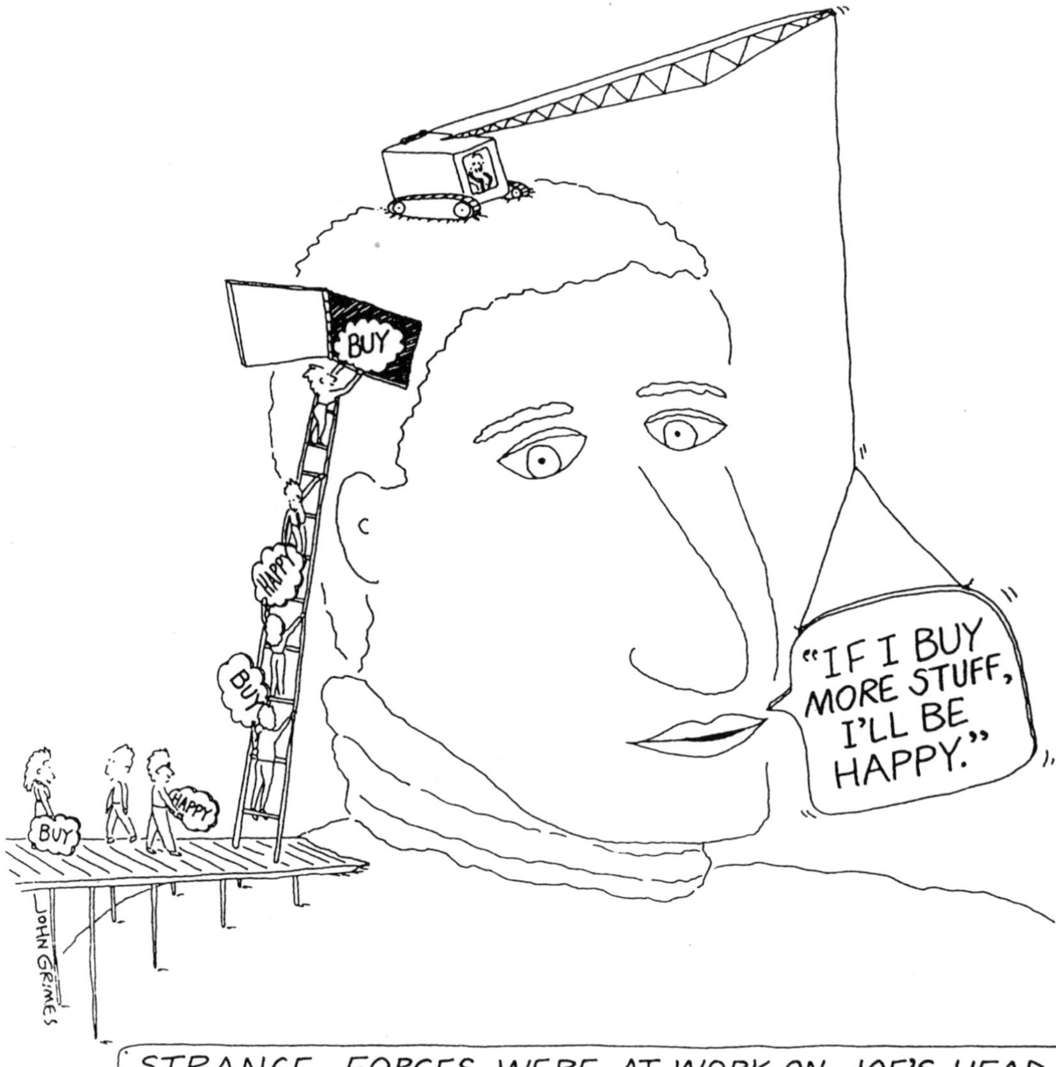
BUY
HAPPY
BUY
BUY
HAPPY
"IF I BUY MORE STUFF, I'LL BE HAPPY."
JOHN GRIMES

STRANGE FORCES WERE AT WORK ON JOE'S HEAD

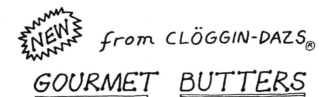

NEW
from CLÖGGIN-DAZS®
GOURMET BUTTERS
CHOCOLATE CHIP
NEAPOLITAN
BUTTER-BARS
(a great source of cholesterol!)
JOHN GRIMES
CLÖGGI

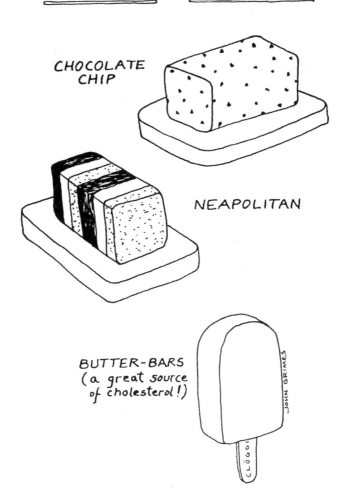

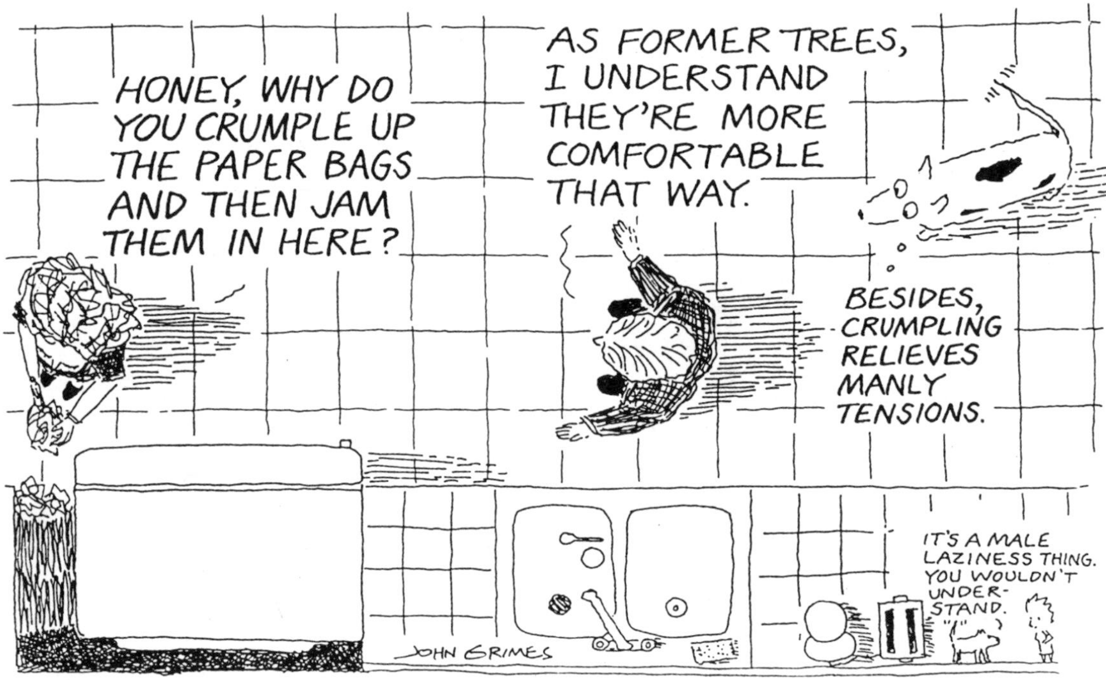
HONEY, WHY DO YOU CRUMPLE UP THE PAPER BAGS AND THEN JAM THEM IN HERE?
AS FORMER TREES, I UNDERSTAND THEY'RE MORE COMFORTABLE THAT WAY.
BESIDES, CRUMPLING RELIEVES MANLY TENSIONS.
IT'S A MALE LAZINESS THING. YOU WOULDN'T UNDER-STAND.
JOHN GRIMES

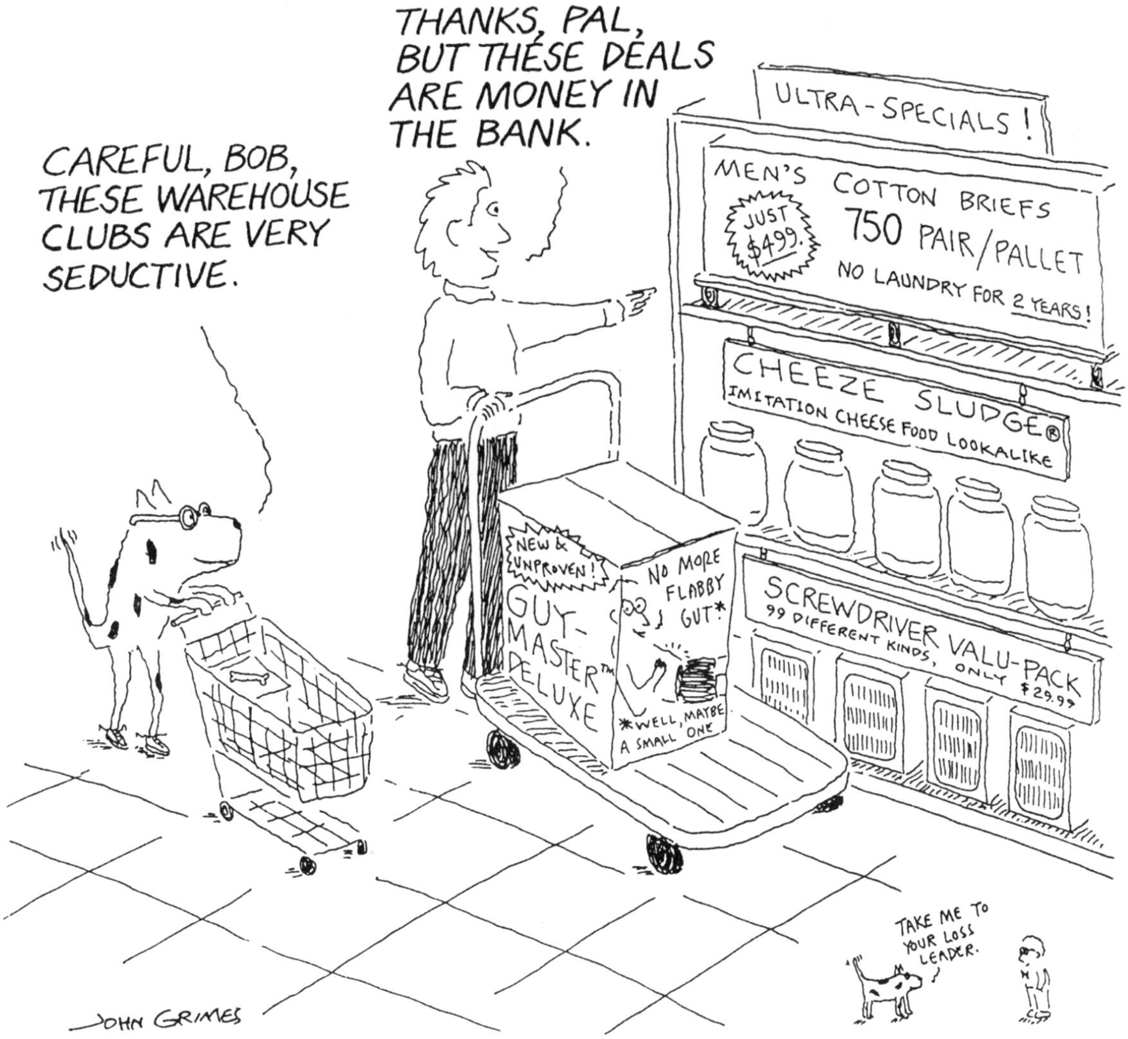
CAREFUL, BOB, THESE WAREHOUSE CLUBS ARE VERY SEDUCTIVE.
THANKS, PAL, BUT THESE DEALS ARE MONEY IN THE BANK.
ULTRA-SPECIALS!
MEN'S COTTON BRIEFS
JUST $499.
750 PAIR/PALLET
NO LAUNDRY FOR 2 YEARS!
CHEEZE SLUDGE®
IMITATION CHEESE FOOD LOOKALIKE
SCREWDRIVER VALU-PACK
99 DIFFERENT KINDS, ONLY $29.99
NEW & UNPROVEN!
GUY-MASTER™ DELUXE
NO MORE FLABBY GUT*
*WELL, MAYBE A SMALL ONE
TAKE ME TO YOUR LOSS LEADER.
JOHN GRIMES

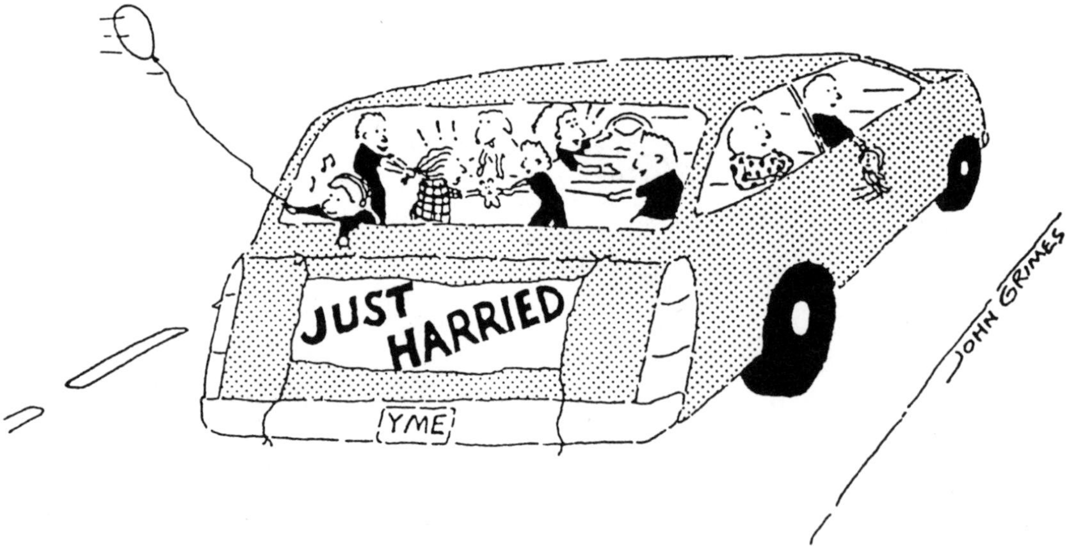

JUST HARRIED
YME
JOHN GRIMES

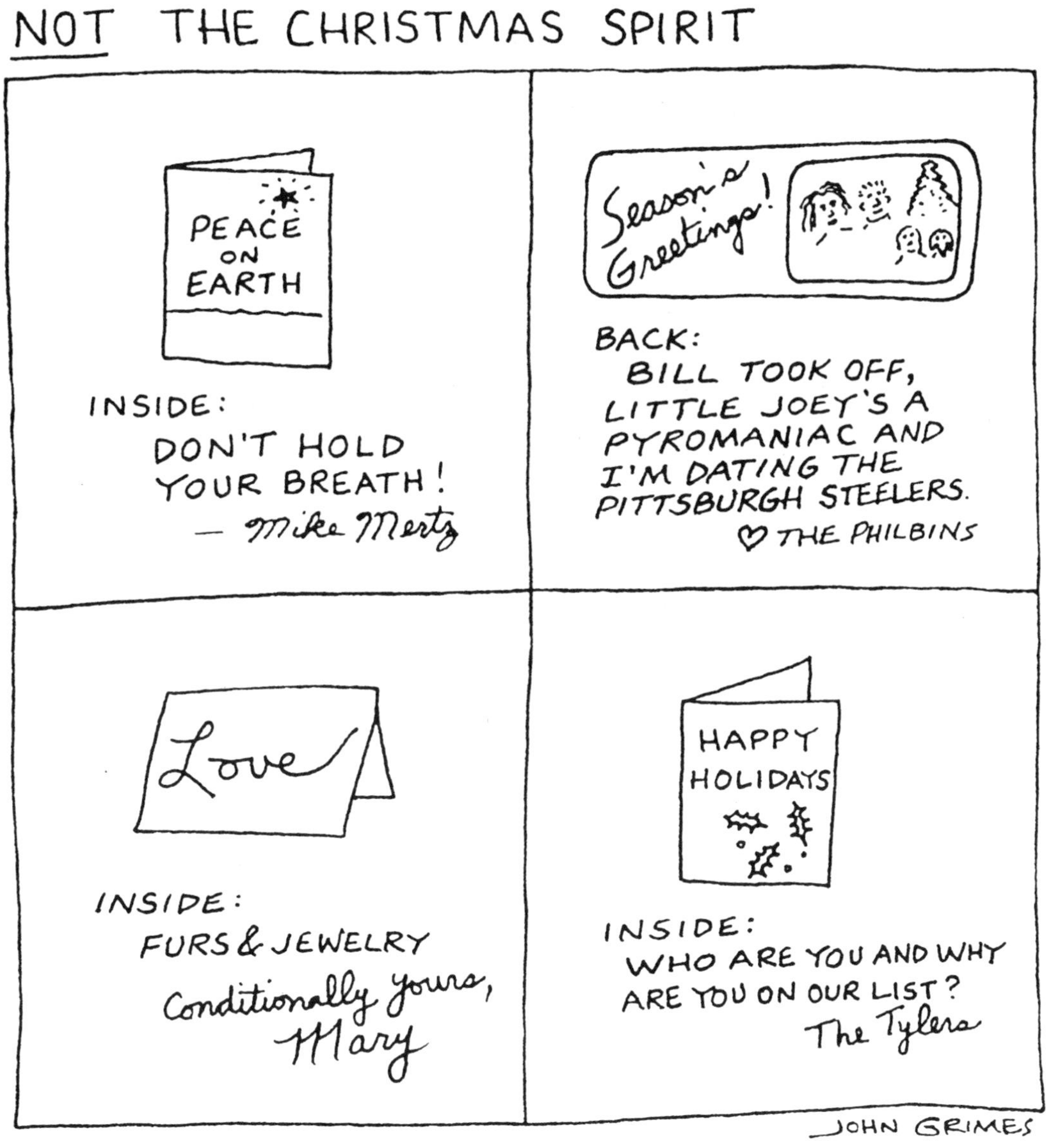
NOT THE CHRISTMAS SPIRIT
PEACE ON EARTH
INSIDE:
DON'T HOLD YOUR BREATH!
— Mike Mertz
Season's Greetings!
BACK:
BILL TOOK OFF, LITTLE JOEY'S A PYROMANIAC AND I'M DATING THE PITTSBURGH STEELERS.
♡ THE PHILBINS
Love
INSIDE:
FURS & JEWELRY
Conditionally yours,
Mary
HAPPY HOLIDAYS
INSIDE:
WHO ARE YOU AND WHY ARE YOU ON OUR LIST?
The Tylers
JOHN GRIMES

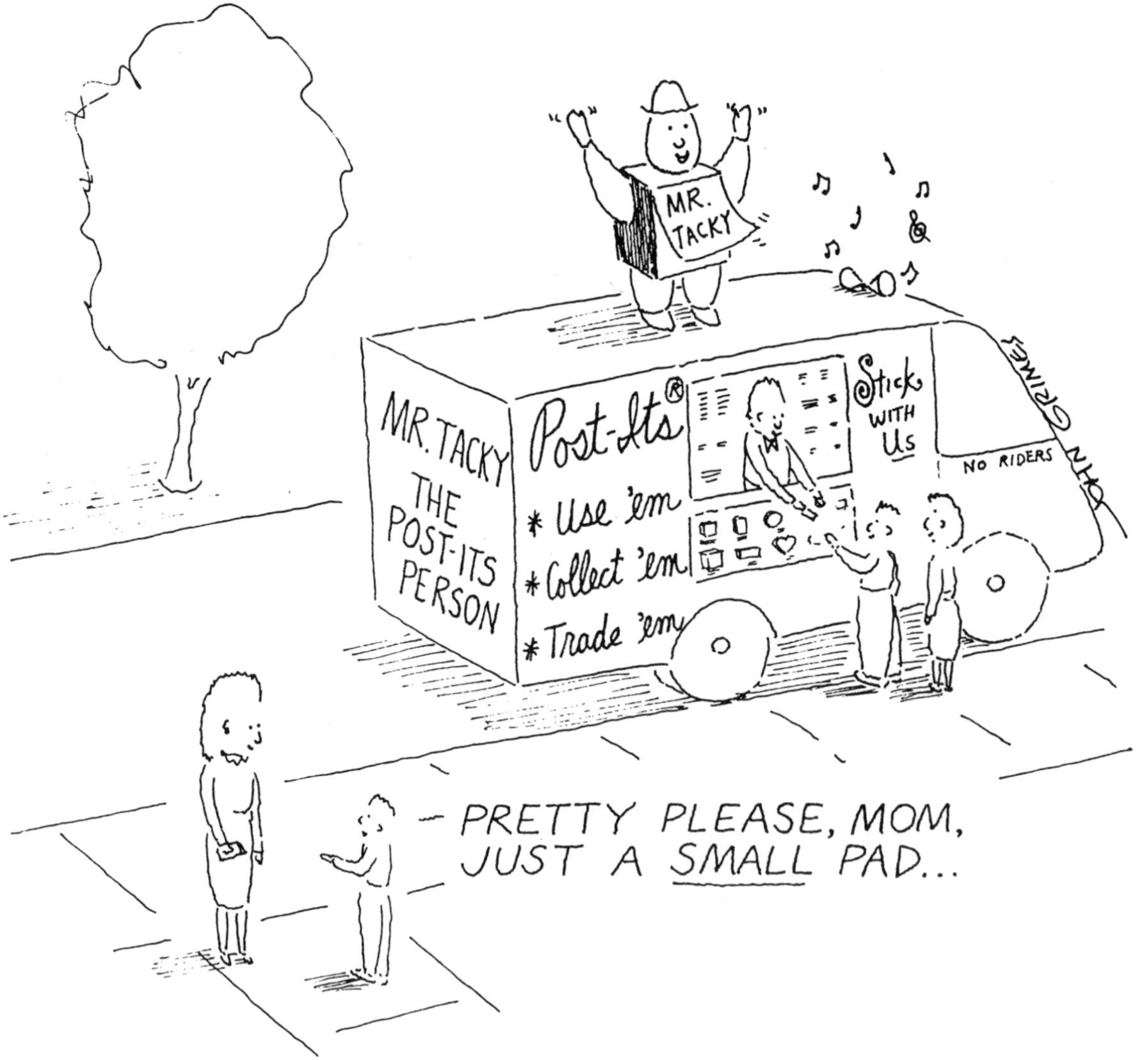
MR. TACKY
MR. TACKY THE POST-ITS PERSON
Post-Its®
* Use 'em
* Collect 'em
* Trade 'em
Stick WITH Us
NO RIDERS
JOHN GRIMES
—PRETTY PLEASE, MOM, JUST A SMALL PAD...

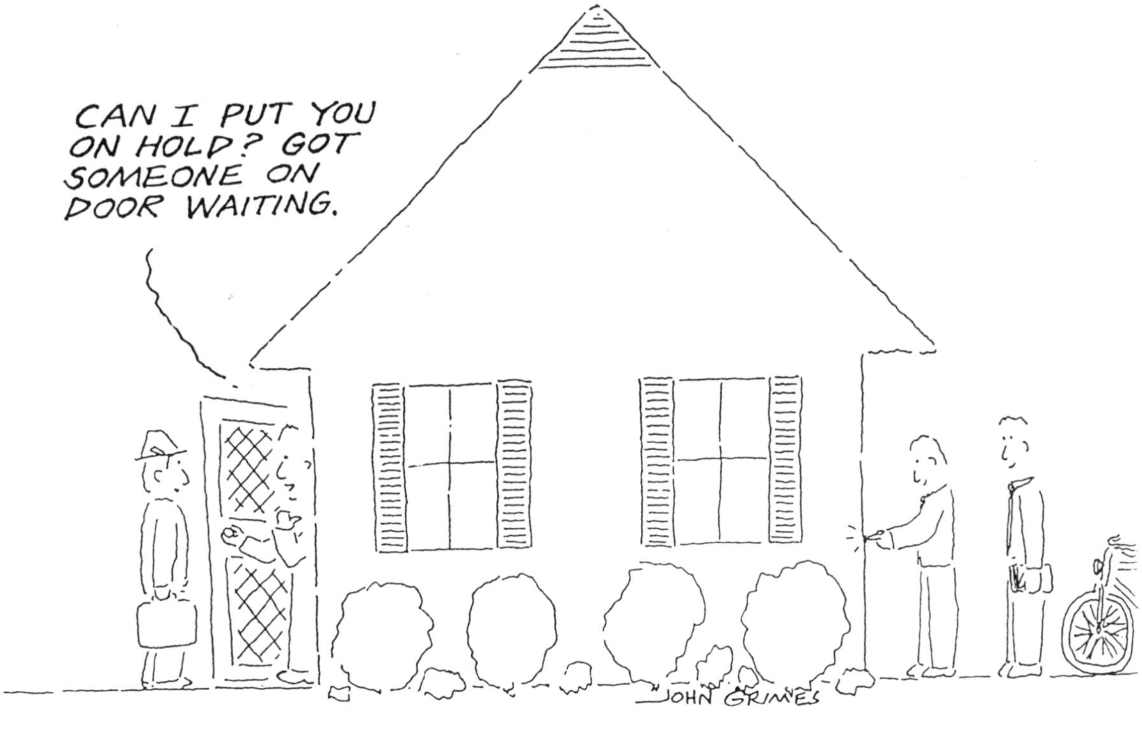
CAN I PUT YOU ON HOLD? GOT SOMEONE ON DOOR WAITING.
JOHN GRIMES

PLEASE!
OFFICIAL
CITY
SOUVENIRS
DOLLS $5
BALLOONS $10
JOHN GRIMES

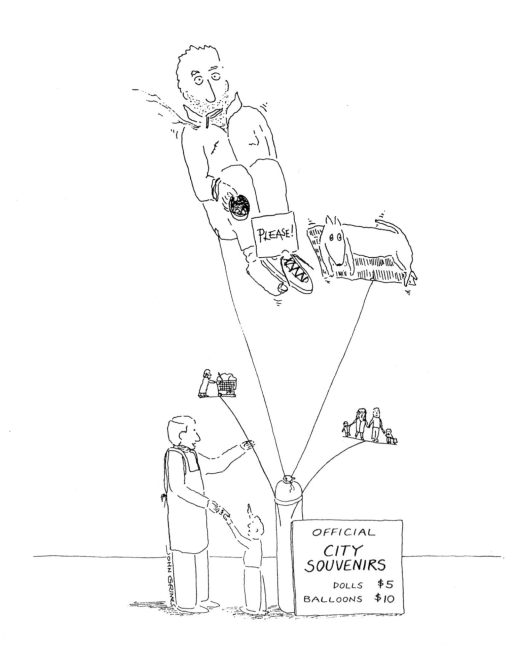

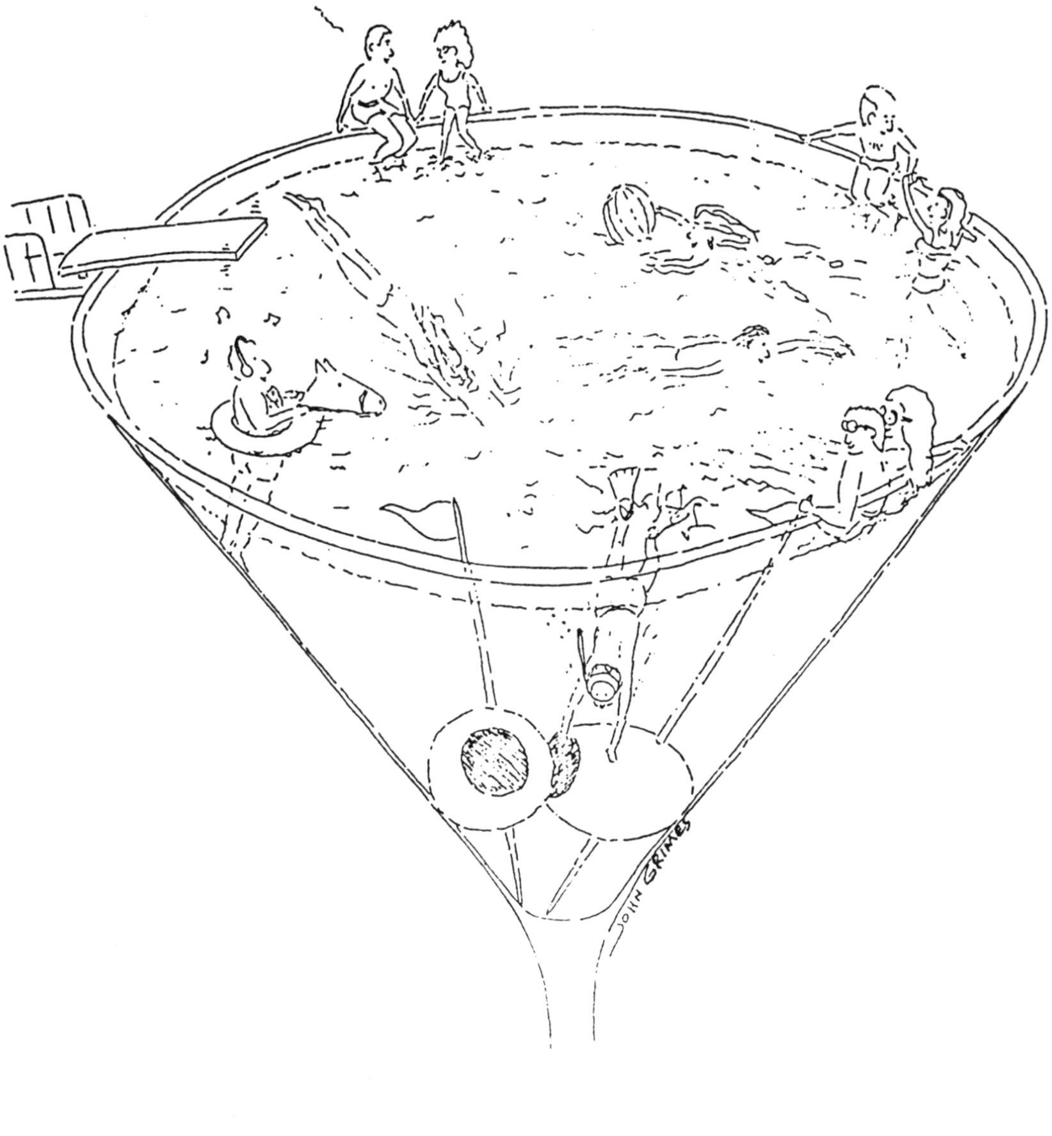
JOHN GRIMES

NOW <u>THIS</u> IS AN OPEN BAR!

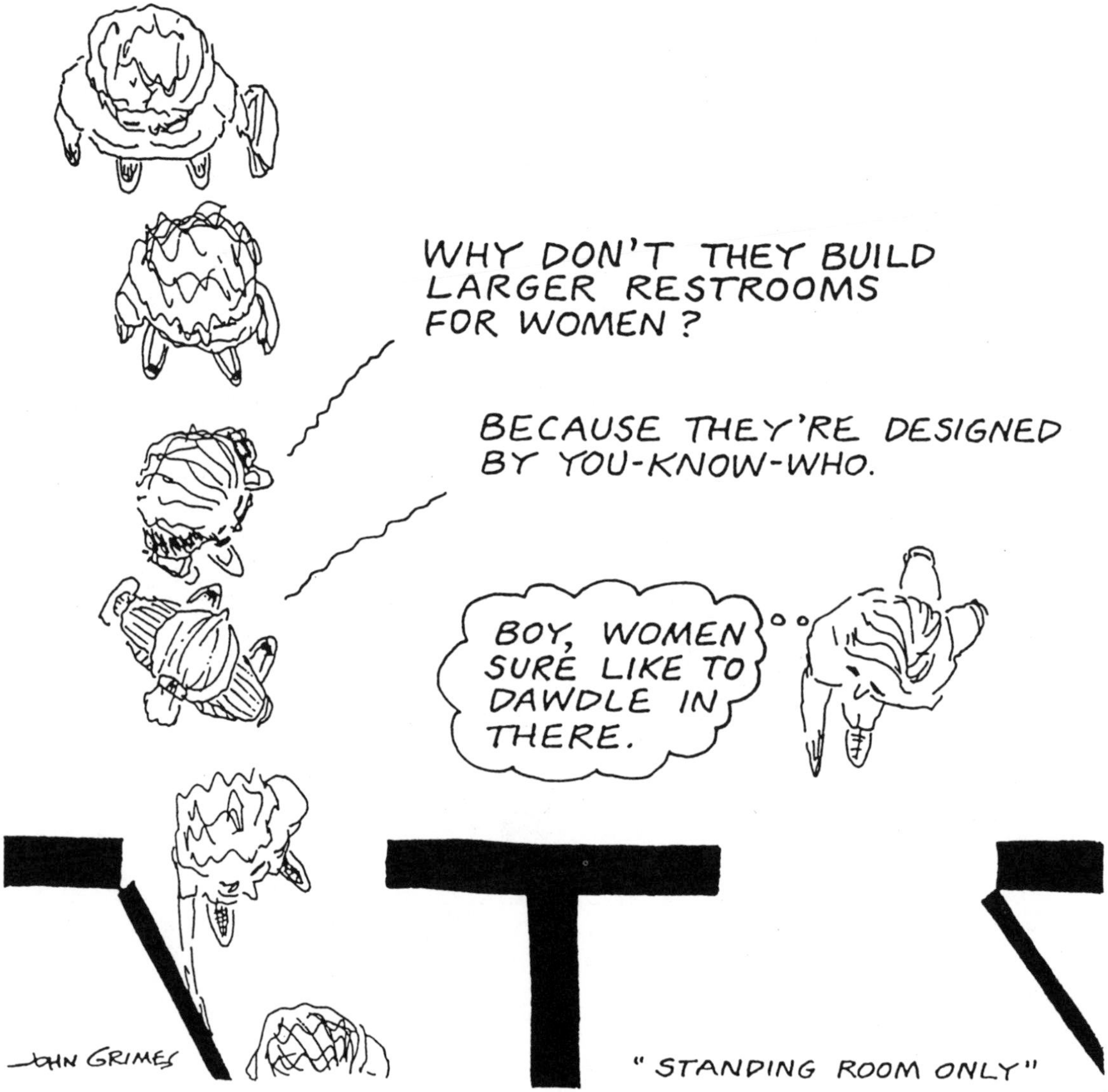
WHY DON'T THEY BUILD LARGER RESTROOMS FOR WOMEN?
BECAUSE THEY'RE DESIGNED BY YOU-KNOW-WHO.
BOY, WOMEN SURE LIKE TO DAWDLE IN THERE.
JOHN GRIMES
"STANDING ROOM ONLY"

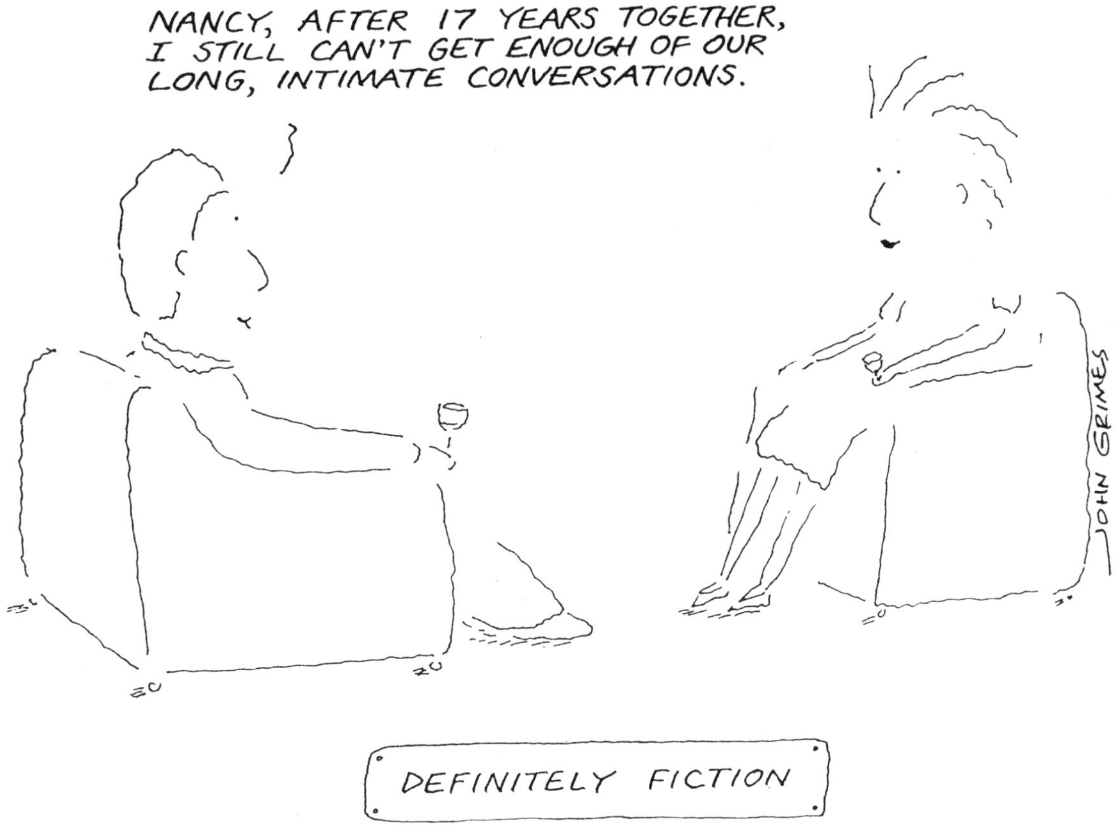
NANCY, AFTER 17 YEARS TOGETHER, I STILL CAN'T GET ENOUGH OF OUR LONG, INTIMATE CONVERSATIONS.
JOHN GRIMES
DEFINITELY FICTION

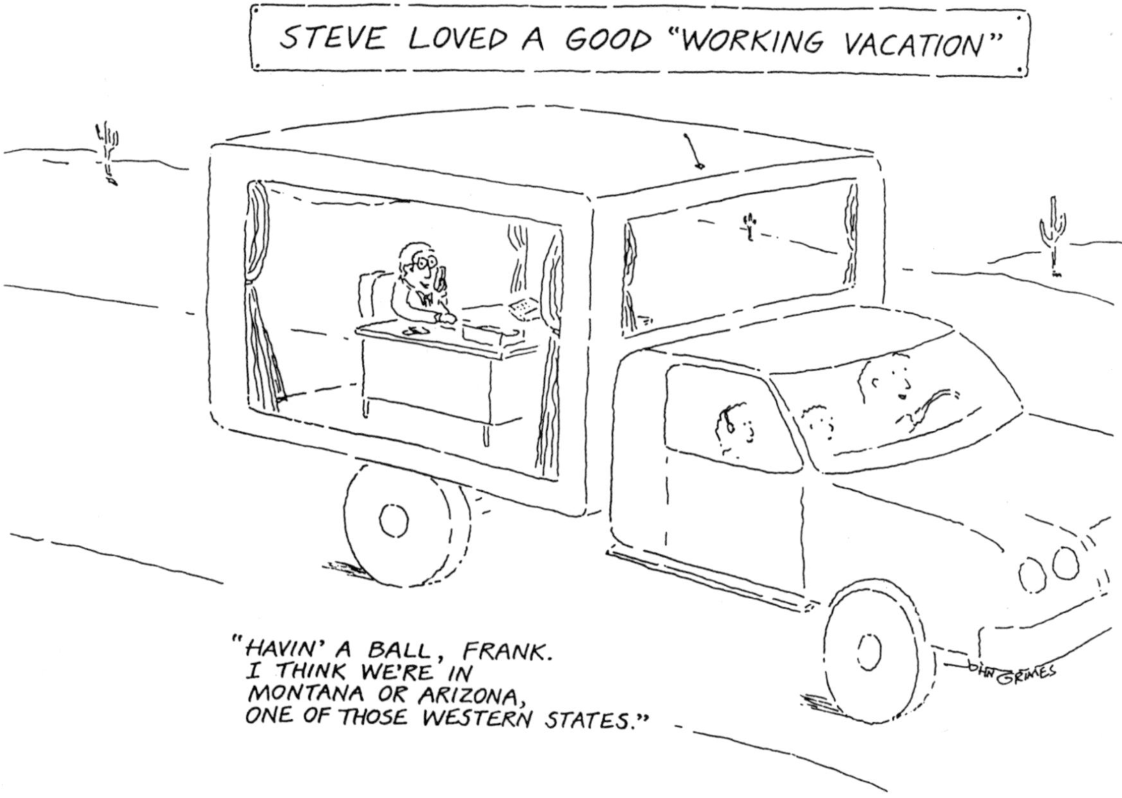
STEVE LOVED A GOOD "WORKING VACATION"
"HAVIN' A BALL, FRANK. I THINK WE'RE IN MONTANA OR ARIZONA, ONE OF THOSE WESTERN STATES."

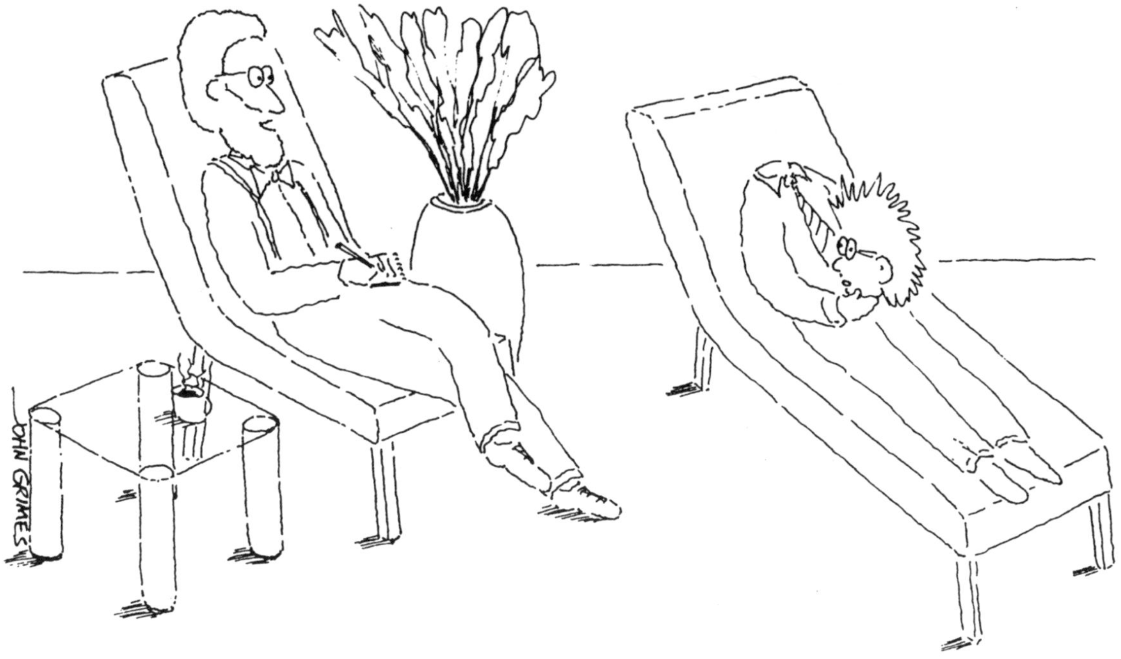
JOHN GRIMES

"STEPHEN, YOU HAVE SOME SERIOUS PROBLEMS, NOT THE LEAST OF WHICH IS THAT SILLY HAIRCUT."

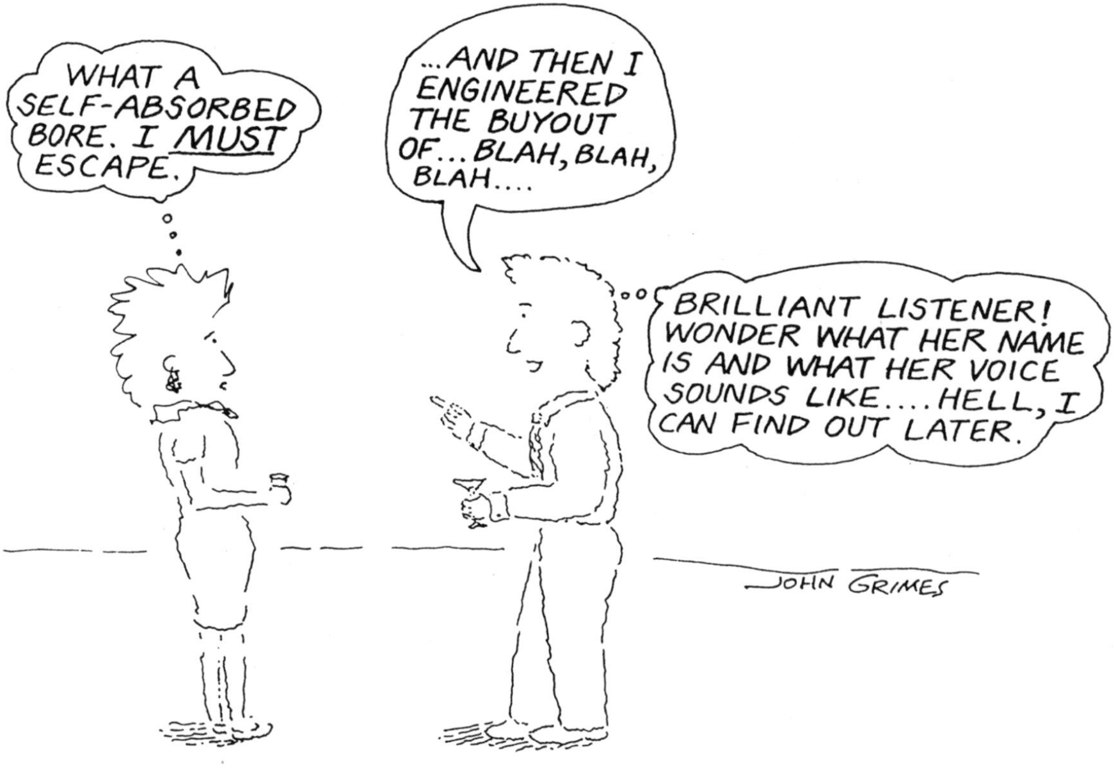
WHAT A SELF-ABSORBED BORE. I MUST ESCAPE.
...AND THEN I ENGINEERED THE BUYOUT OF...BLAH, BLAH, BLAH....
BRILLIANT LISTENER! WONDER WHAT HER NAME IS AND WHAT HER VOICE SOUNDS LIKE....HELL, I CAN FIND OUT LATER.
JOHN GRIMES

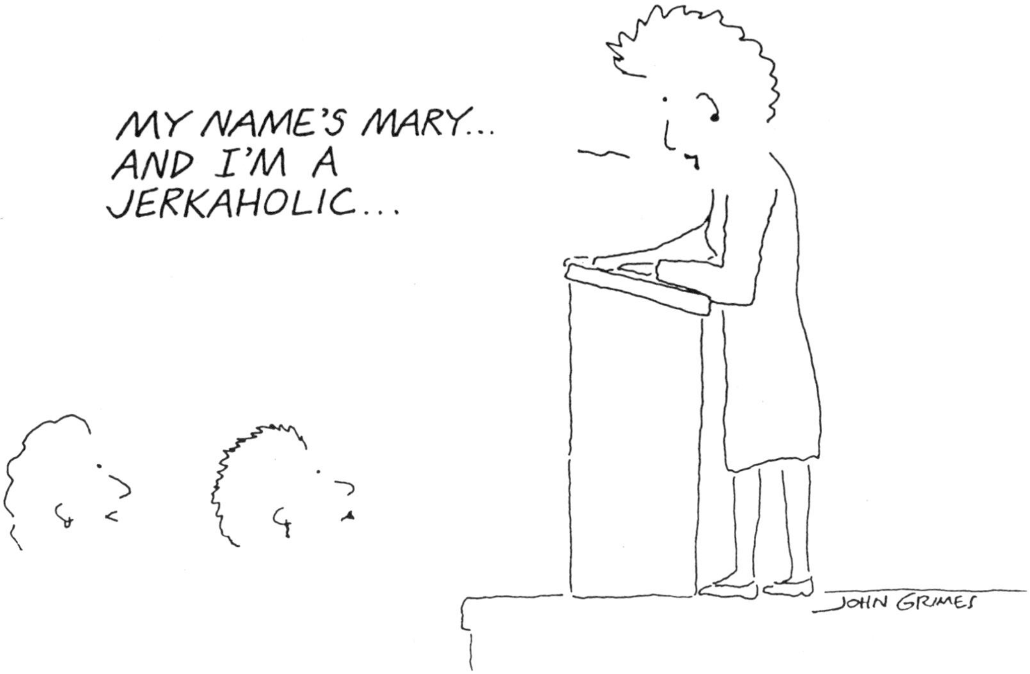
MY NAME'S MARY...
AND I'M A
JERKAHOLIC...
JOHN GRIMES

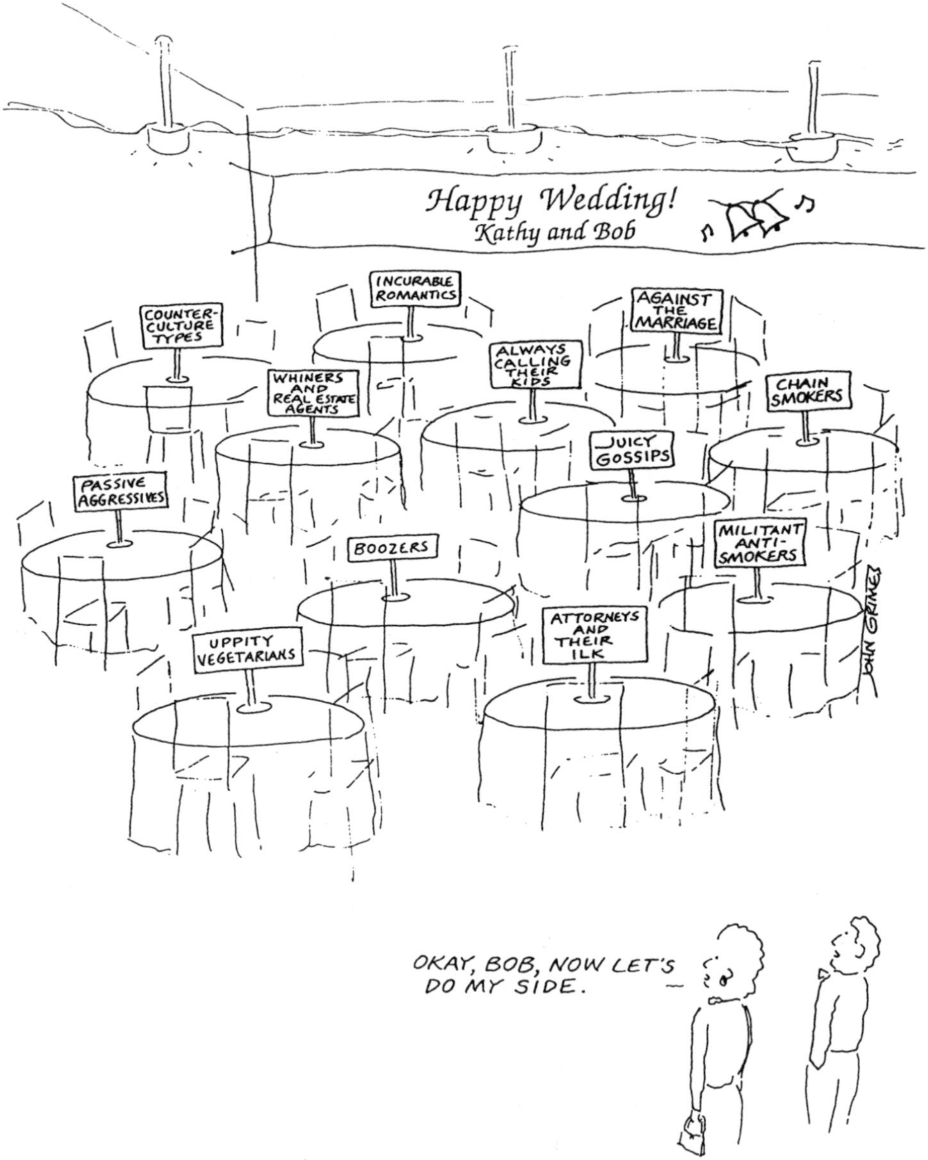
Happy Wedding!
Kathy and Bob
COUNTER-CULTURE TYPES
INCURABLE ROMANTICS
AGAINST THE MARRIAGE
ALWAYS CALLING THEIR KIDS
WHINERS AND REAL ESTATE AGENTS
CHAIN SMOKERS
JUICY GOSSIPS
PASSIVE AGGRESSIVES
BOOZERS
MILITANT ANTI-SMOKERS
ATTORNEYS AND THEIR ILK
UPPITY VEGETARIANS
JOHN GRIMES
OKAY, BOB, NOW LET'S DO MY SIDE.

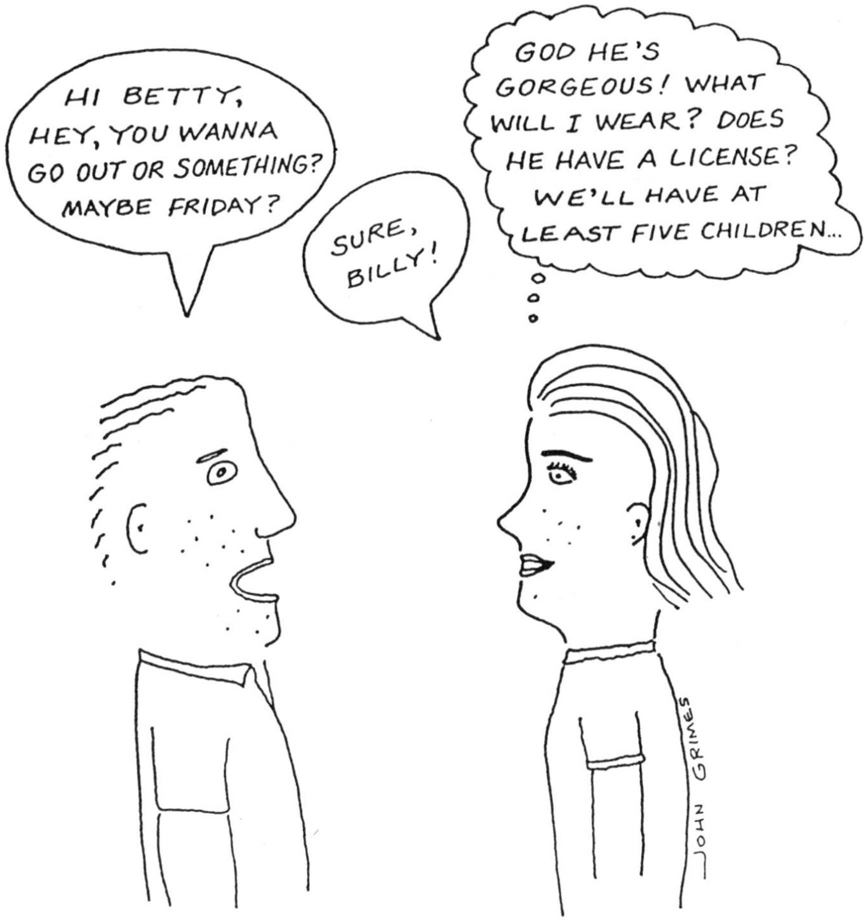
HI BETTY, HEY, YOU WANNA GO OUT OR SOMETHING? MAYBE FRIDAY?
SURE, BILLY!
GOD HE'S GORGEOUS! WHAT WILL I WEAR? DOES HE HAVE A LICENSE? WE'LL HAVE AT LEAST FIVE CHILDREN...
JOHN GRIMES

BEFORE WOMEN WISED UP

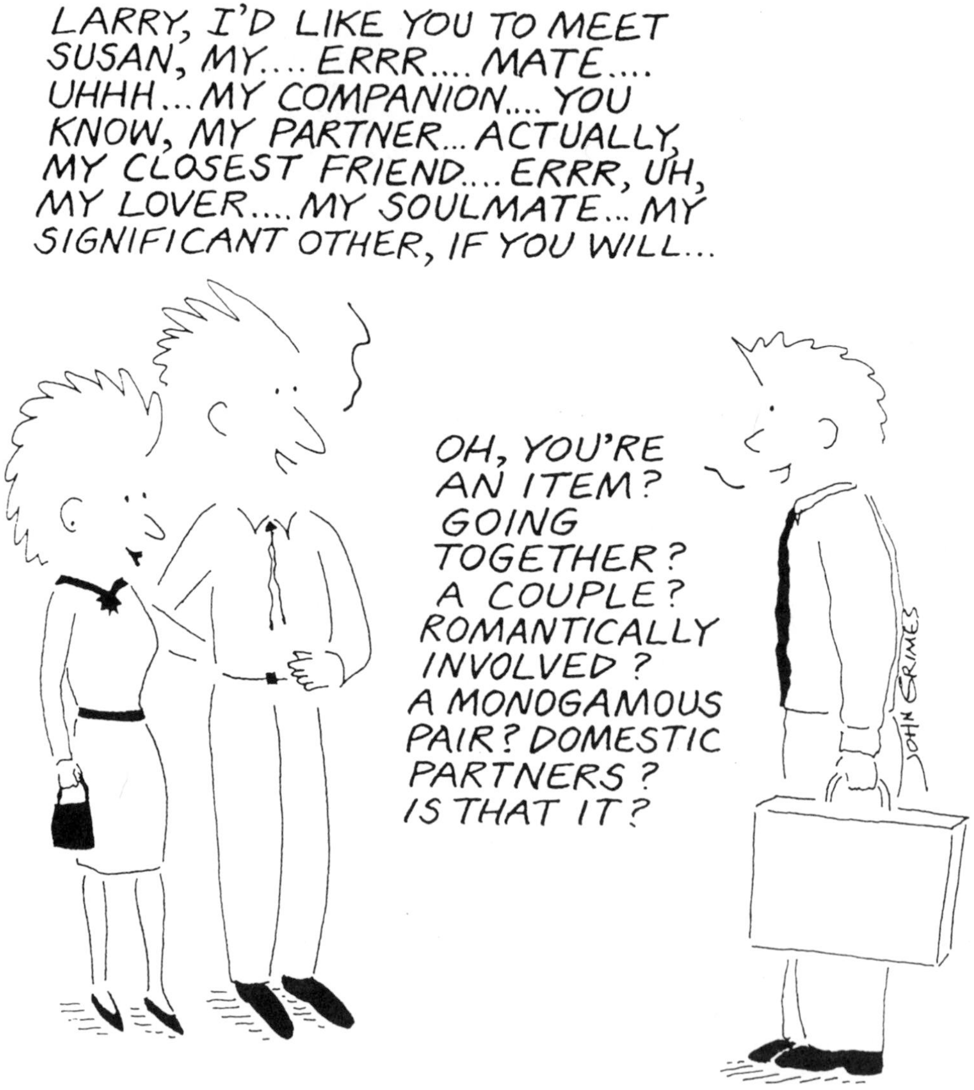
LARRY, I'D LIKE YOU TO MEET SUSAN, MY.... ERRR.... MATE.... UHHH... MY COMPANION.... YOU KNOW, MY PARTNER... ACTUALLY, MY CLOSEST FRIEND.... ERRR, UH, MY LOVER.... MY SOULMATE... MY SIGNIFICANT OTHER, IF YOU WILL...
OH, YOU'RE AN ITEM? GOING TOGETHER? A COUPLE? ROMANTICALLY INVOLVED? A MONOGAMOUS PAIR? DOMESTIC PARTNERS? IS THAT IT?
JOHN GRIMES

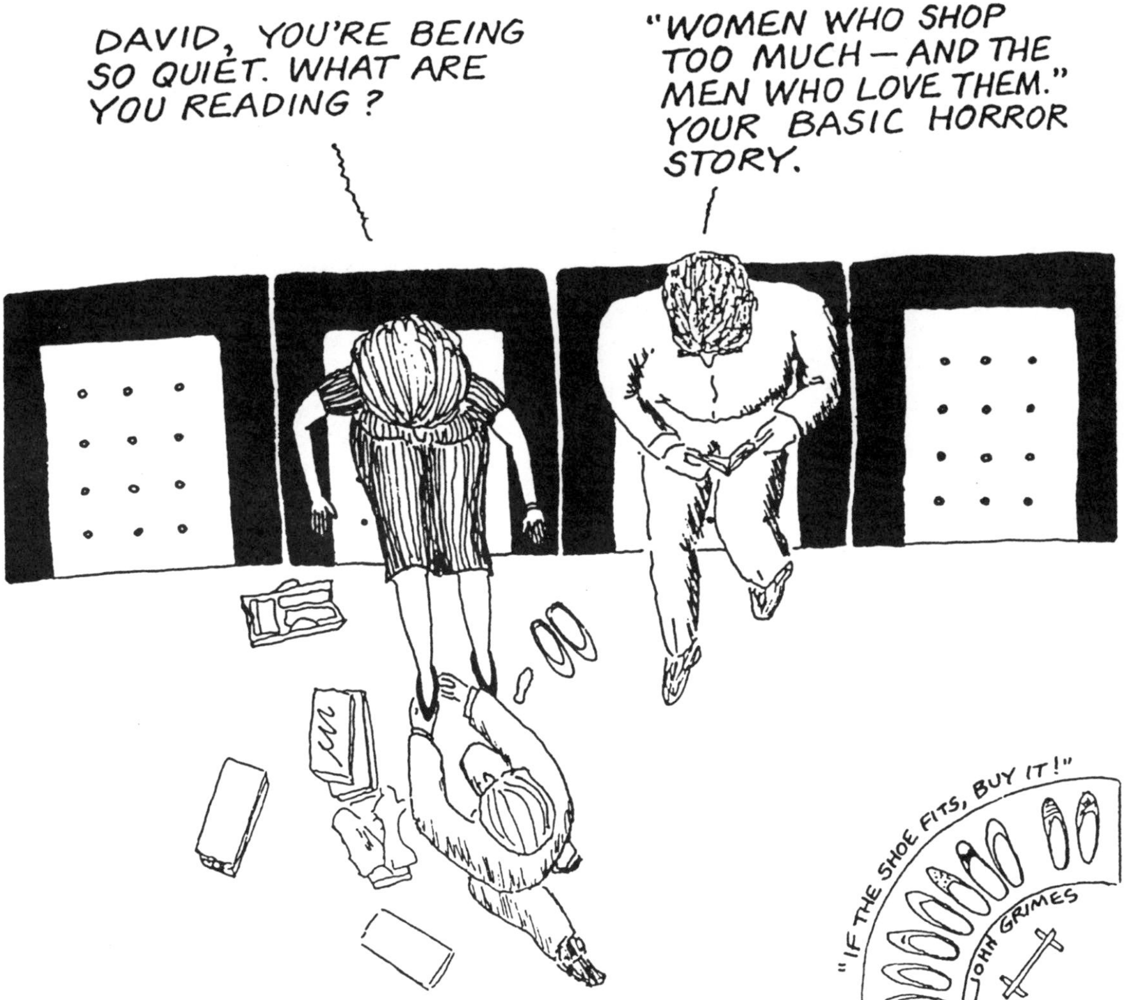
DAVID, YOU'RE BEING SO QUIET. WHAT ARE YOU READING?
"WOMEN WHO SHOP TOO MUCH—AND THE MEN WHO LOVE THEM." YOUR BASIC HORROR STORY.
"IF THE SHOE FITS, BUY IT!"
JOHN GRIMES

AVERAGING ONLY $38 A YEAR AS A FREELANCE WRITER, LARRY BEGINS THE PAINFUL PROCESS OF LAYING HIMSELF OFF.

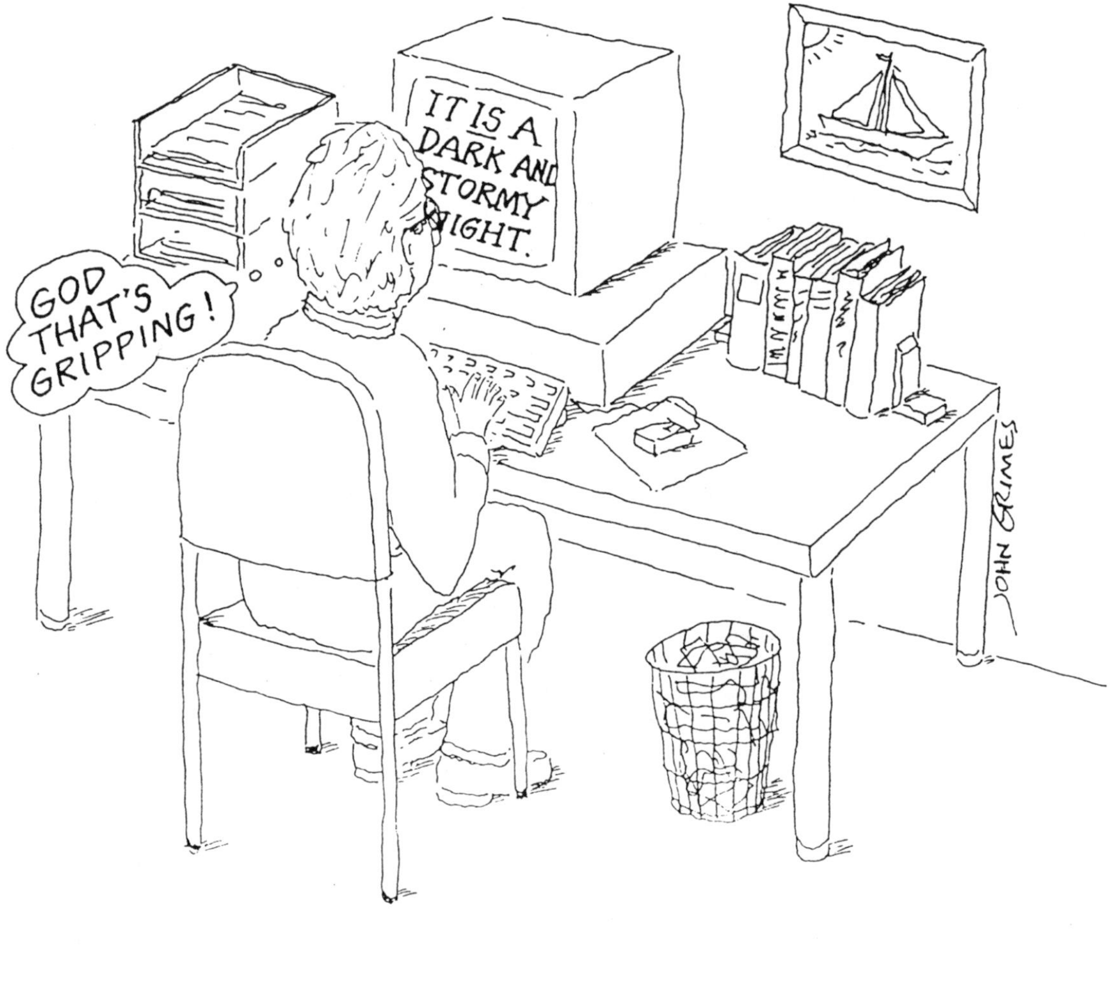
IT IS A
DARK AN
STORMY
IGHT.
GOD THAT'S GRIPPING!
JOHN GRIMES

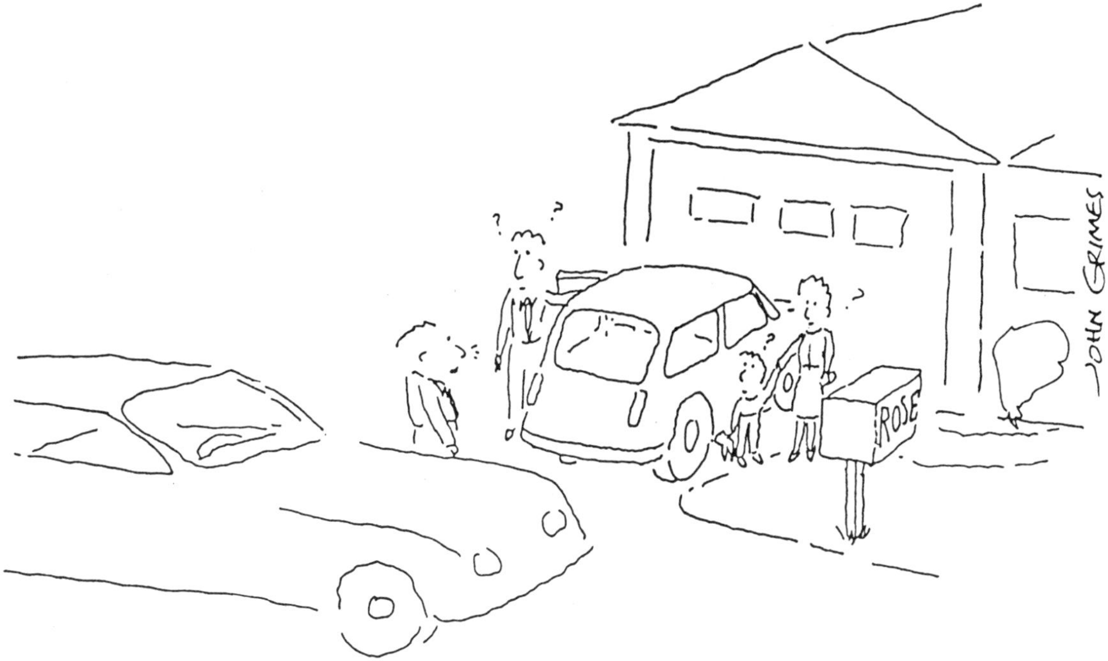
ROSE
JOHN GRIMES

CAUGHT UP IN THE RAT RACE,
TED FINALLY DECIDES TO
STOP AND SMELL THE ROSES.

"ON WALL STREET TODAY, GREED & AVARICE LED ALL OTHER VALUES BY A FIVE-TO-ONE MARGIN."

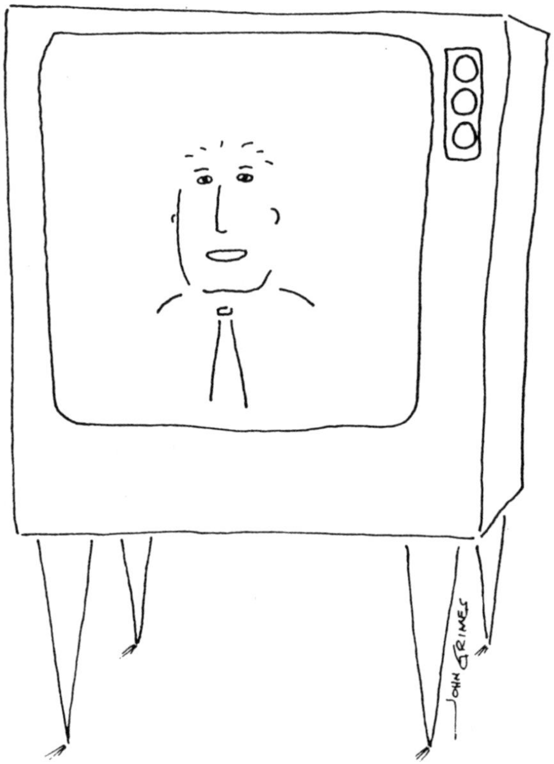
JOHN GRIMES

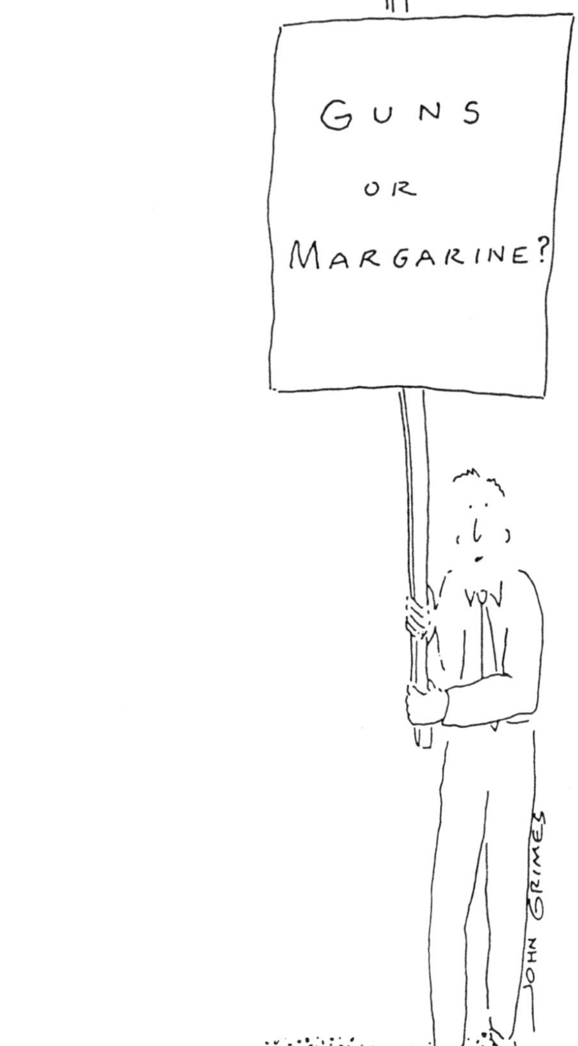
GUNS
OR
MARGARINE?
JOHN GRIMES

HAVING LOST THE CAR MARKET TO JAPAN, DETROIT TRIES ITS HAND AT HOUSING.

WALK-IN CLOSET (GREAT FOR URBAN DEBRIS, CANS, BOTTLES, KIDS AND PETS)
MASTER SUITE (FOR SINGLE PARENTS OR SHORT COUPLES)
TO EXIT, SCREAM LOUDLY
PRIVATE REC ROOM (ACCOMMODATES 2-4 MAL-NOURISHED CHILDREN)
HEAVY GUAGE PLASTIC SHEETING
SECURE STORAGE OR KITCHEN-ETTE
SECURITY SYSTEM (OPTIONAL)
EMACIATED MUTT (OPTIONAL)
MOBILITY PODS (OPTIONAL)
PORTABLE FOUNDATION
BATHROOM/GROCERY CART STORAGE AREA (NOT INCLUDED; CONSULT LOCAL AUTHORITIES)
OHN GRIMES

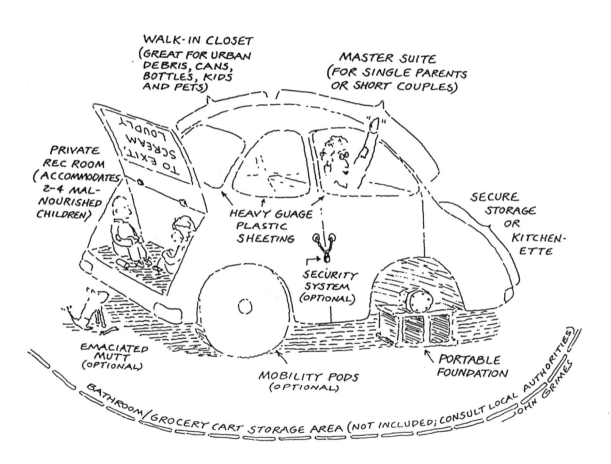

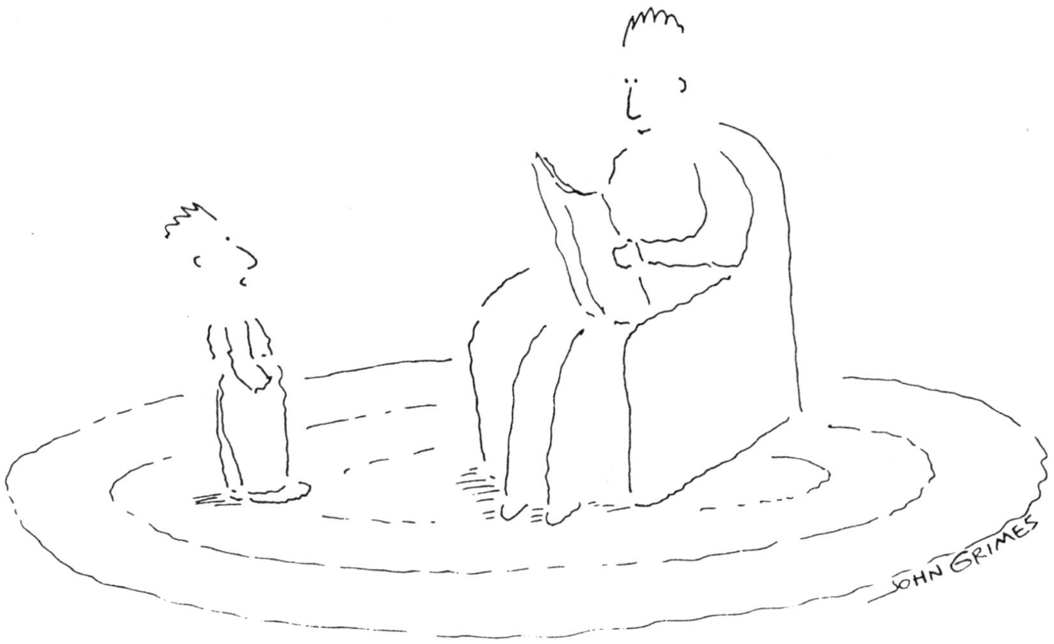
JOHN GRIMES

"DAD, WHAT'S A PEACE DIVIDEND?"

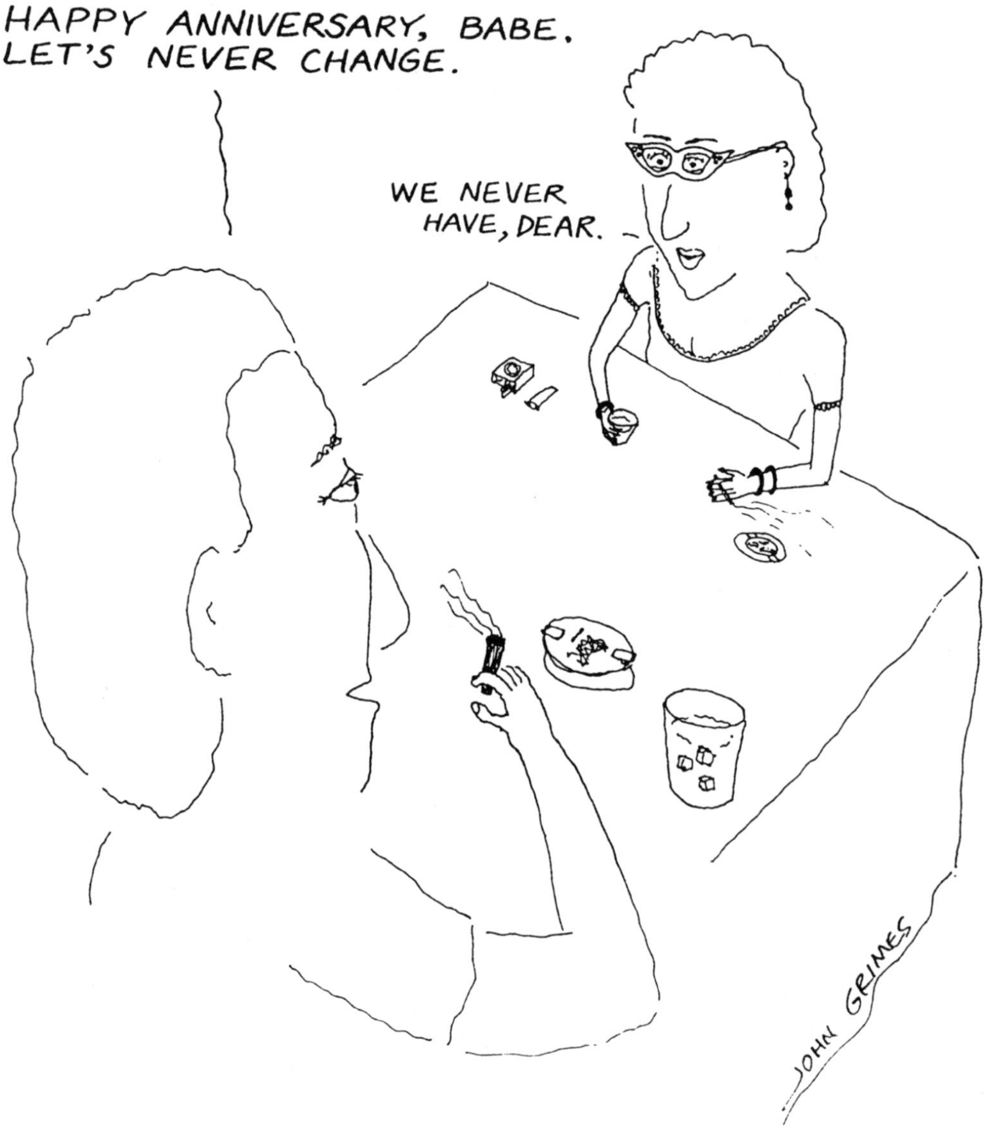
HAPPY ANNIVERSARY, BABE.
LET'S NEVER CHANGE.
WE NEVER
HAVE, DEAR.
JOHN GRIMES

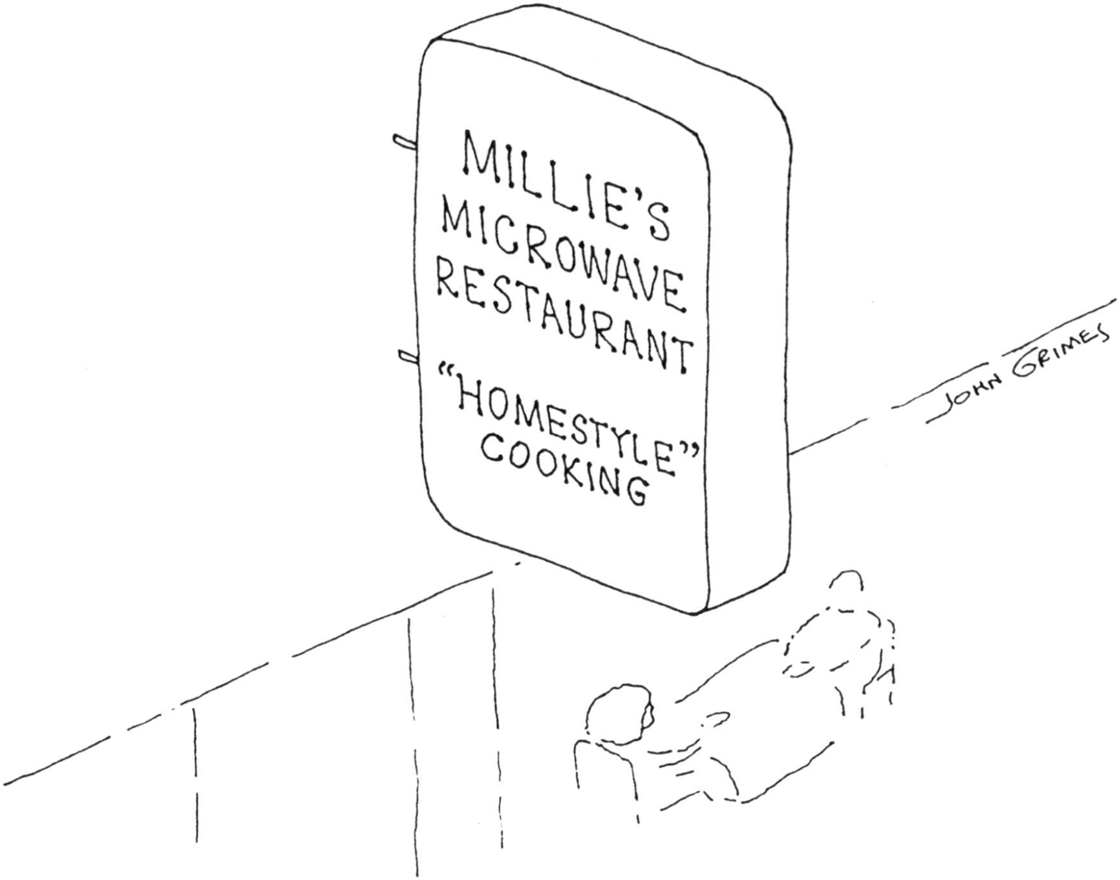
MILLIE'S
MICROWAVE
RESTAURANT
"HOMESTYLE"
COOKING
JOHN GRIMES

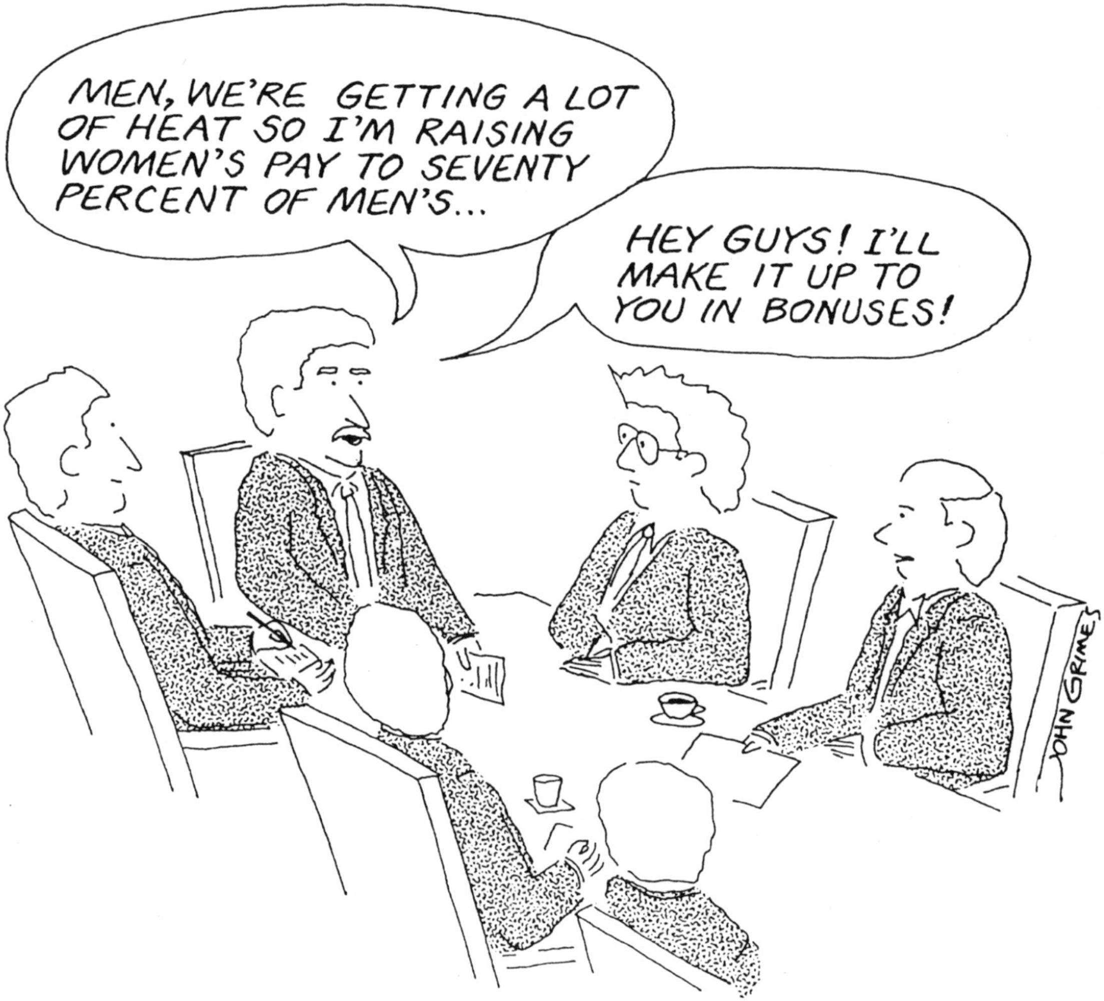
MEN, WE'RE GETTING A LOT OF HEAT SO I'M RAISING WOMEN'S PAY TO SEVENTY PERCENT OF MEN'S...
HEY GUYS! I'LL MAKE IT UP TO YOU IN BONUSES!
JOHN GRIMES

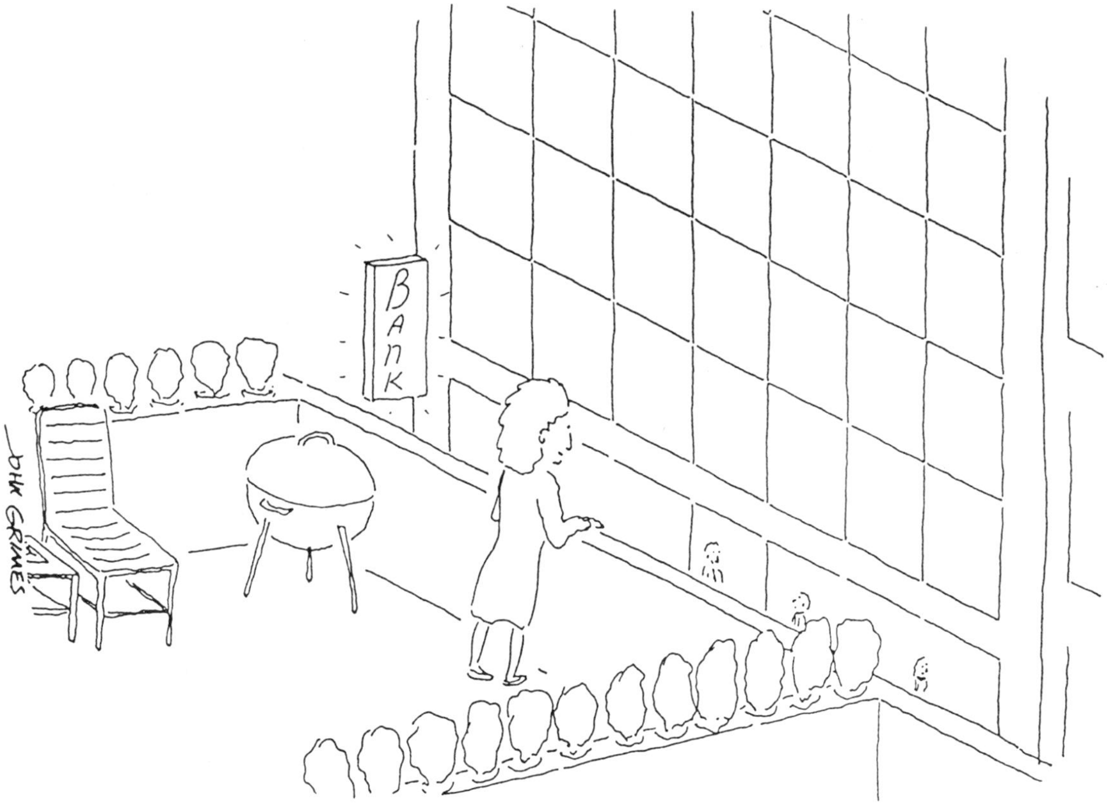
BANK
Dik Grimes

SHE LOOKED DOWN AND THERE THEY WERE,
TWO EX-BOYFRIENDS,
LIKE SHITS THAT PASS IN THE NIGHT.

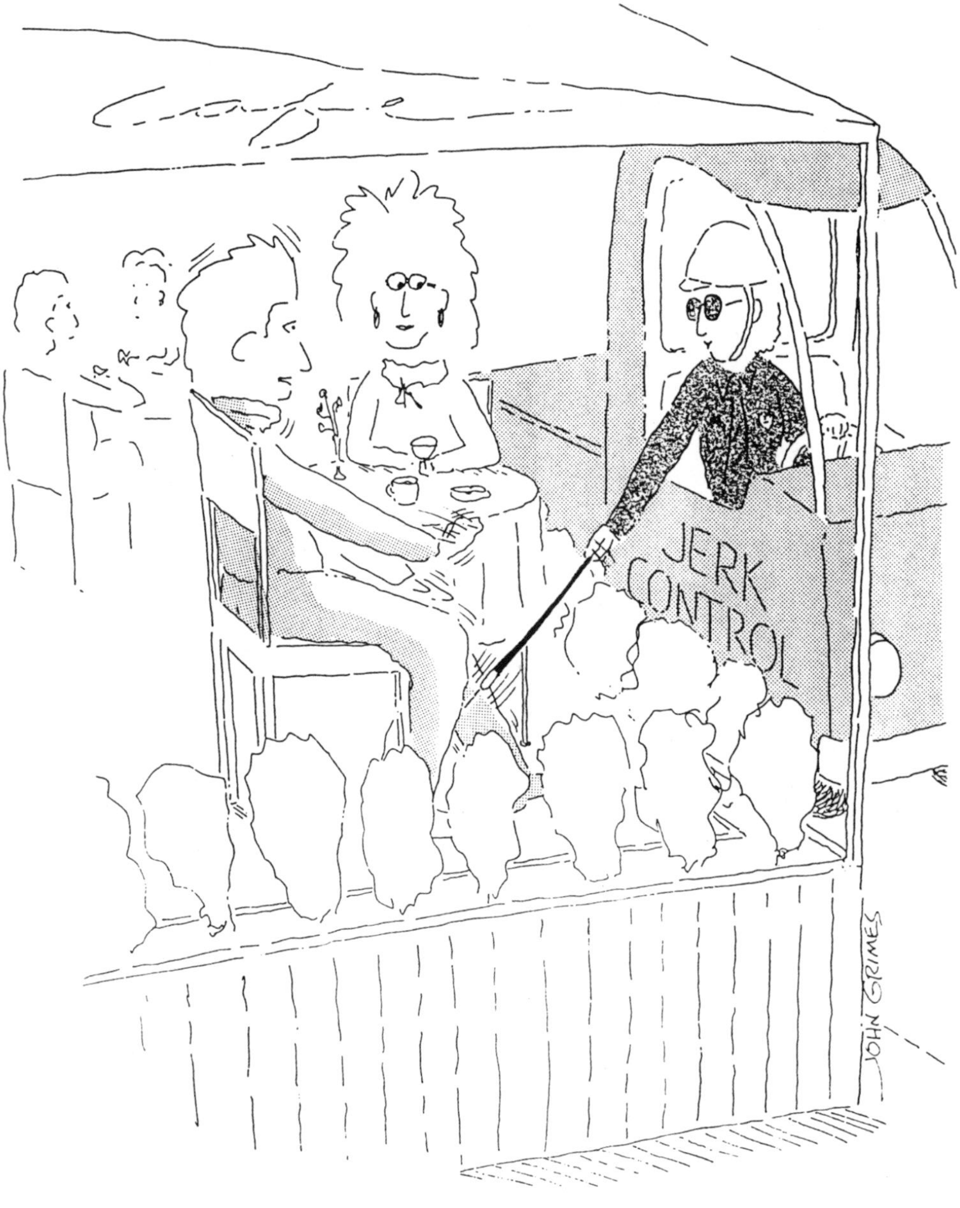
JERK
CONTROL
JOHN GRIMES

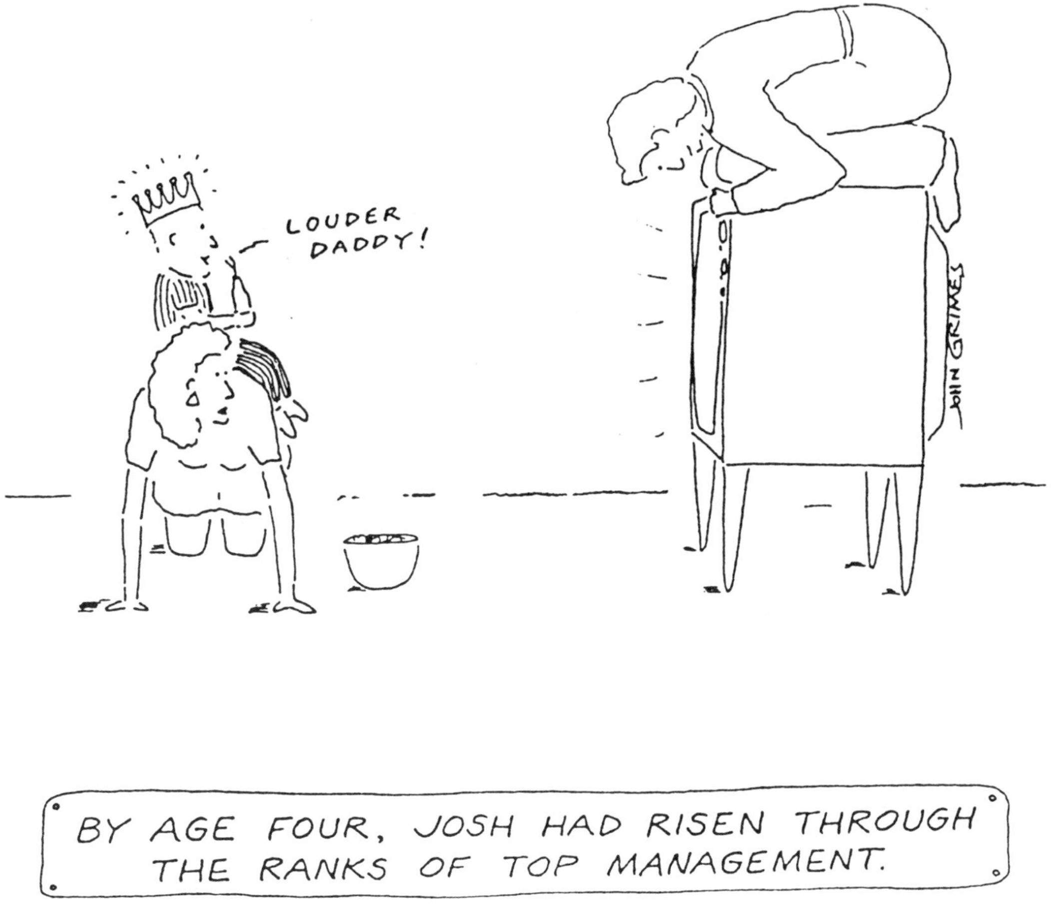
LOUDER DADDY!

BY AGE FOUR, JOSH HAD RISEN THROUGH THE RANKS OF TOP MANAGEMENT.

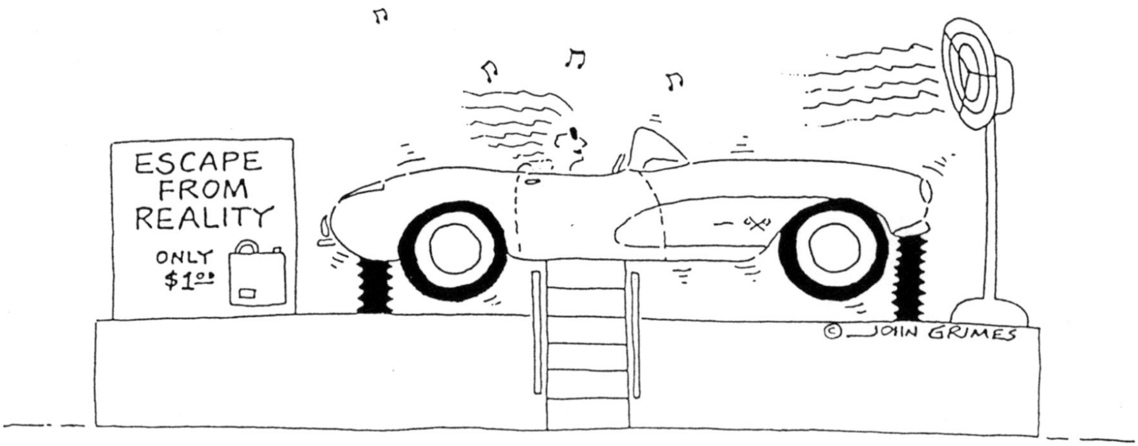
ESCAPE
FROM
REALITY
ONLY
$1.00
© JOHN GRIMES

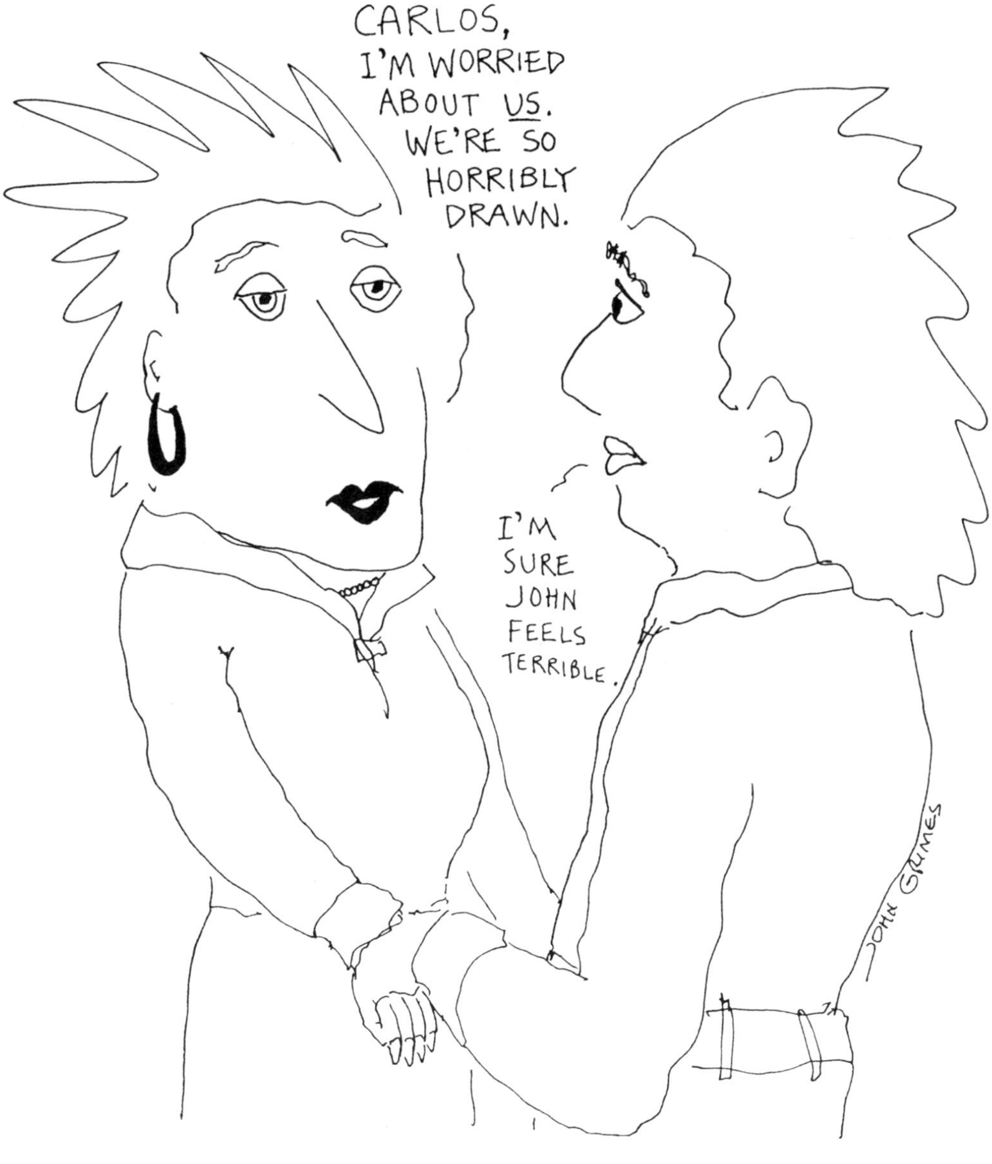
CARLOS, I'M WORRIED ABOUT US. WE'RE SO HORRIBLY DRAWN.
I'M SURE JOHN FEELS TERRIBLE.
JOHN GRIMES

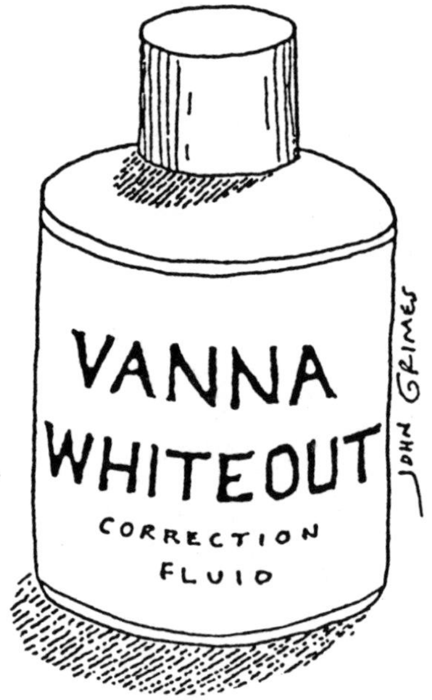
VANNA
WHITEOUT
CORRECTION
FLUID
JOHN GRIMES

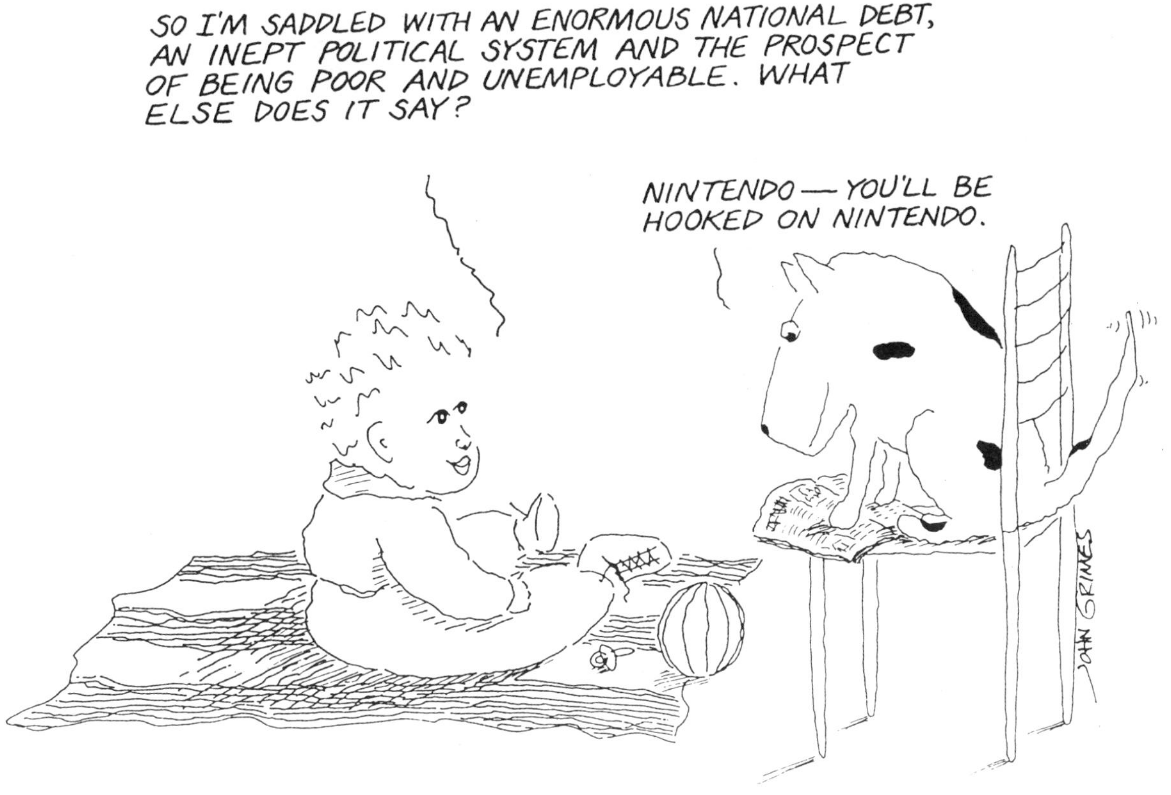
SO I'M SADDLED WITH AN ENORMOUS NATIONAL DEBT, AN INEPT POLITICAL SYSTEM AND THE PROSPECT OF BEING POOR AND UNEMPLOYABLE. WHAT ELSE DOES IT SAY?
NINTENDO — YOU'LL BE HOOKED ON NINTENDO.
JOHN GRIMES

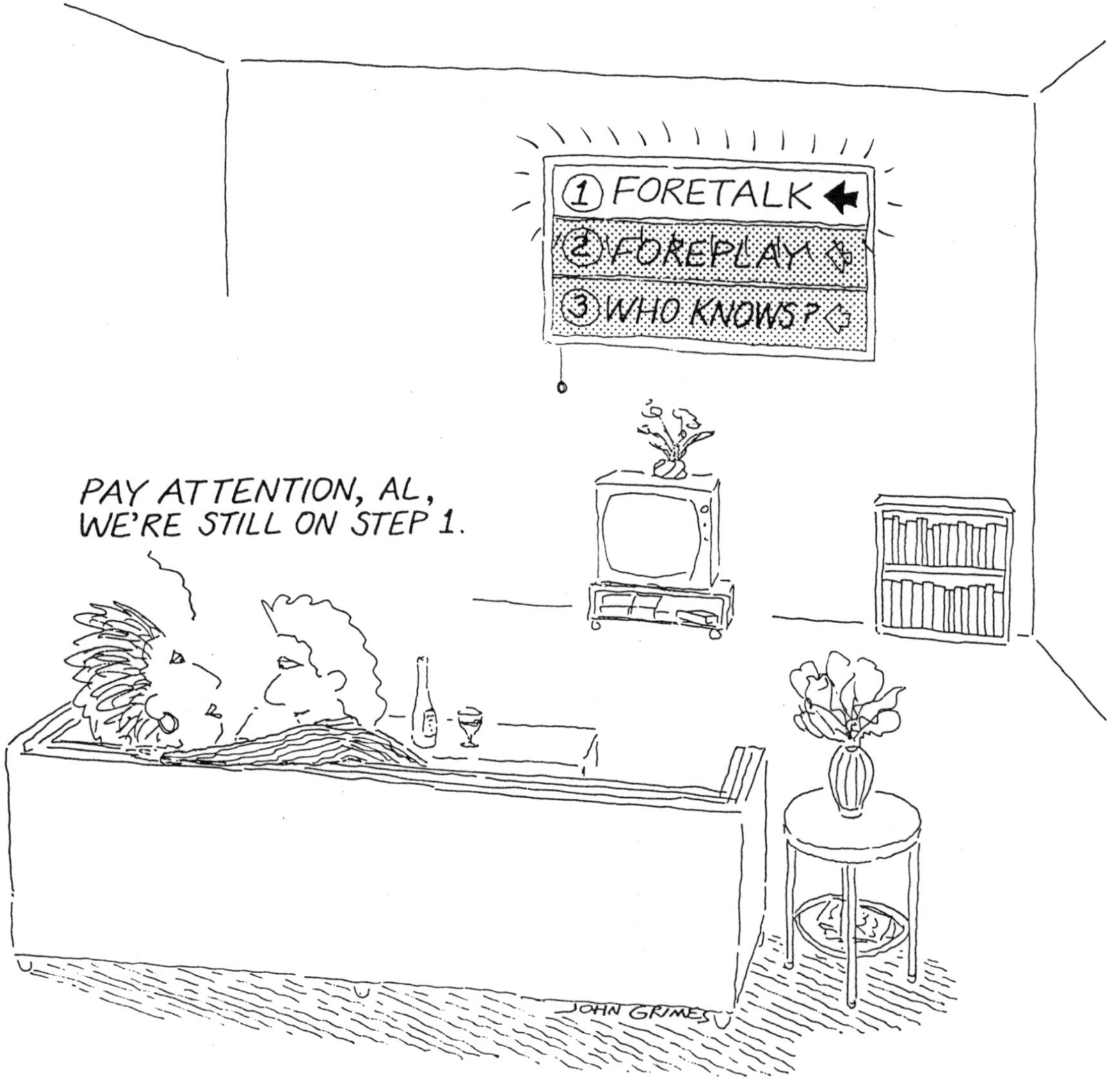
1 FORETALK
2 FOREPLAY
3 WHO KNOWS?
PAY ATTENTION, AL,
WE'RE STILL ON STEP 1.
JOHN GRIMES

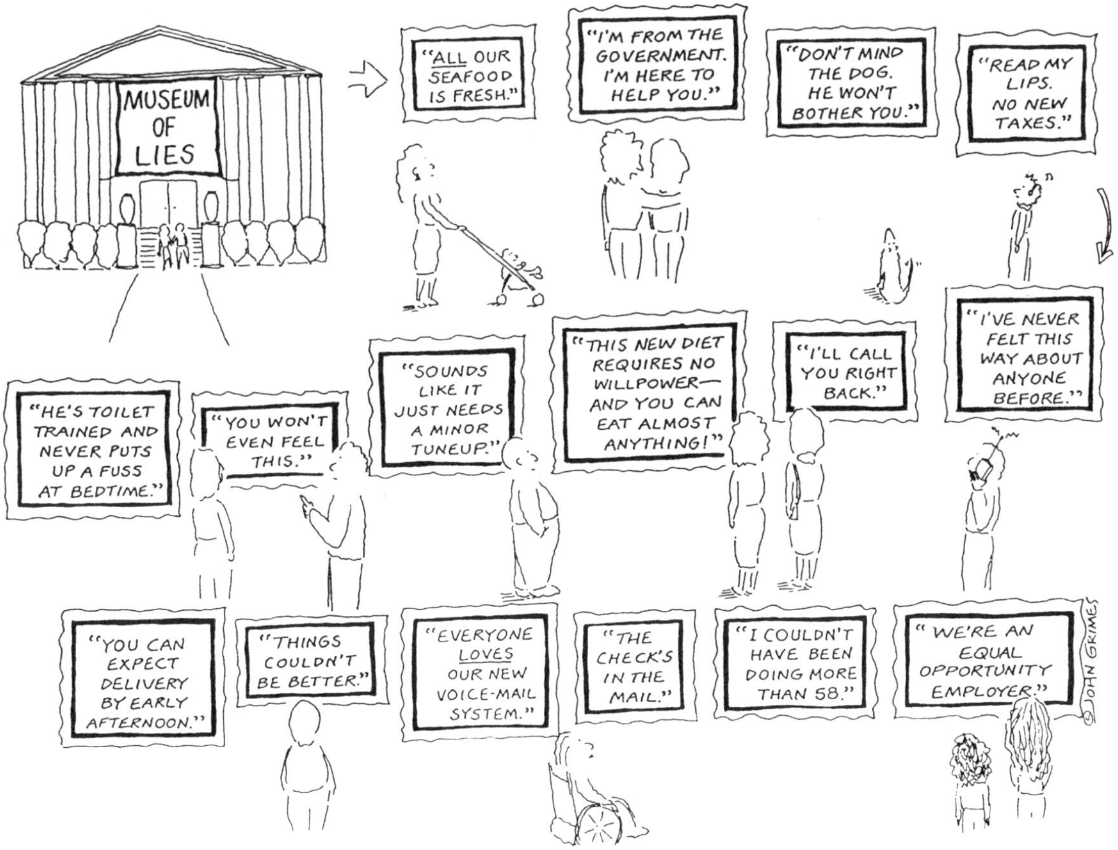
MUSEUM OF LIES
"ALL OUR SEAFOOD IS FRESH."
"I'M FROM THE GOVERNMENT. I'M HERE TO HELP YOU."
"DON'T MIND THE DOG. HE WON'T BOTHER YOU."
"READ MY LIPS. NO NEW TAXES."
"I'VE NEVER FELT THIS WAY ABOUT ANYONE BEFORE."
"I'LL CALL YOU RIGHT BACK."
"THIS NEW DIET REQUIRES NO WILLPOWER— AND YOU CAN EAT ALMOST ANYTHING!"
"SOUNDS LIKE IT JUST NEEDS A MINOR TUNEUP."
"YOU WON'T EVEN FEEL THIS."
"HE'S TOILET TRAINED AND NEVER PUTS UP A FUSS AT BEDTIME."
"YOU CAN EXPECT DELIVERY BY EARLY AFTERNOON."
"THINGS COULDN'T BE BETTER."
"EVERYONE LOVES OUR NEW VOICE-MAIL SYSTEM."
"THE CHECK'S IN THE MAIL."
"I COULDN'T HAVE BEEN DOING MORE THAN 58."
"WE'RE AN EQUAL OPPORTUNITY EMPLOYER."
© JOHN GRIMES

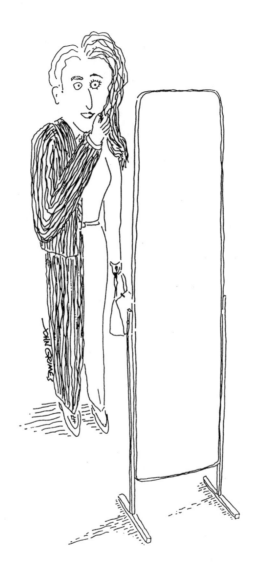

GARY GETS IN TOUCH
WITH HIS FEMININE SIDE.

CROSSING
JOHN GRIMES

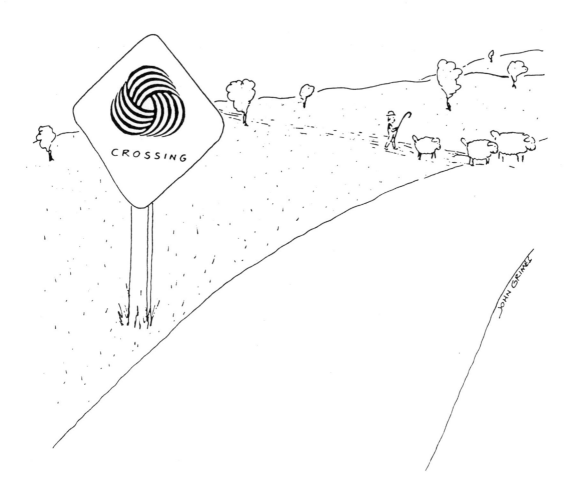

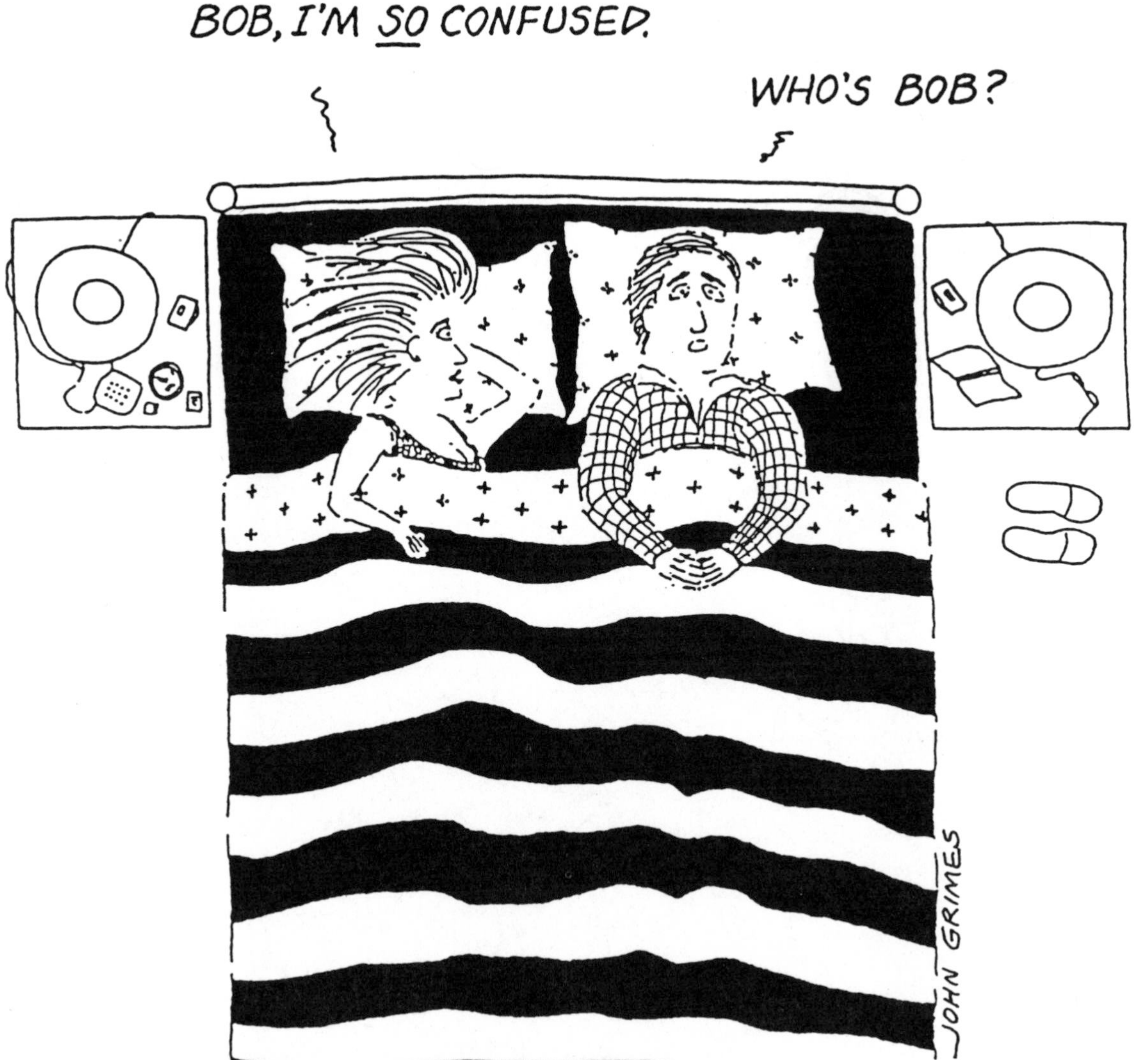
BOB, I'M SO CONFUSED.
WHO'S BOB?
JOHN GRIMES